The Illustrated
ATLAS
of the
UNITED STATES

The Illustrated
ATLAS
of the
UNITED STATES

Keith Lye

Regency House ⬮ Publishing Ltd.

Published in 1997 by
REGENCY HOUSE PUBLISHING LIMITED
3 Mill Lane, Broxbourne,
Hertfordshire EN10 7AZ
United Kingdom

Copyright © 1997 Regency House
Publishing Limited

ISBN 1 85361 452 1

Printed in Italy

Maps drawn by Clive Spong
Flags supplied by © the Flag Research Center and Lovell Johns Ltd.
Photographs: Life File pages 2, 3, 6 both, 7 both, 12, 14, 15, 17, 18-19, 20, 22, 23, 24, 25, 27, 28-29, 30,
31, 32-33, 34, 35, 36, 37, 40, 48, 51, 62, 63, 64, 65, 66-67, 68, 69, 70, 71, 72-73, 74, 75, 76, 77, 78.
Telegraph Picture Library pages 13, 16, 21, 26, 38, 39, 42, 43, 44, 49, 50, 52, 53, 54, 55, 57, 58.
Comstock pages 45, 56, 59

Front cover: map of California.
Back cover: detail from map of Texas.

Page 2: Statue of Liberty, New York.
Page 3: Bryce Canyon National Park, Utah.

Contents

Introduction

The United States is one of the world's largest countries. Because of its great size, it has an almost infinite variety of climates and landscapes, ranging from the frozen Arctic wastes of northern Alaska to the sunny beaches of Florida, the hot deserts of the southwest, and the tropical islands of Hawaii in the North Pacific Ocean. In the early 16th century the country was largely a wilderness, with a population of perhaps 18 million Native Americans living in Canada and the United States. Even today, when the population has exceeded the 260 million mark, the country still has vast areas almost empty of people, including snow-capped

mountain ranges, parched desert basins, great rivers, and vast plains that stretch as far as the eye can see.

Many scenic features, such as Arizona's Grand Canyon, California's Yosemite Valley, and Wyoming's Old Faithful geyser, now protected within national parks, are among the world's most magnificent natural wonders and the creation of national parks in the United States has been an inspiration to conservationists worldwide. As the great American naturalist John Muir observed in 1898, "wildness is a necessity" and "parks and reservations are useful not only as fountains of timber and irrigating rivers, but as fountains of life." They are places where people, especially those seeking occasional refuge from the bustle of the cities, can obtain spiritual renewal through contact with nature.

A number of America's most impressive landmarks were created by people. Between the 11th and 13th centuries, Native Americans, called the Anasazi, built cliff dwellings on canyon walls, such as those of the Mesa Verde National Park, Colorado, while their descendants, the Pueblo, built settlements such as Acoma, in New Mexico, that date back to the 14th century. From the 16th century, early pioneers from Europe also

resources to become one of the world's most highly developed countries. In doing so, it pioneered industrial techniques, such as moving assembly lines and automation, while it has also advanced the frontiers of medicine, science, and technology and leads the world in many areas of scientific enquiry. Perhaps the best known achievements in recent times are the manned and unmanned voyages of discovery launched by NASA to the Moon and beyond to the distant regions of the Solar system. NASA's work has greatly increased our understanding of the complexities of the Universe.

The Illustrated Atlas of the United States is a state-by-state guide to this great country. It contains maps of the 50 states, plus the capital Washington, D.C. Information about the states accompanies each map, together with state flags, climate charts, and descriptions of the land and its economy. The text also highlights major attractions for visitors, including important natural, cultural, historical, and recreational features, while tables of dates outline key events in the state's history.

played a part in the founding of towns.

The oldest permanent settlement in the United States, St. Augustine, Florida, which was founded by a Spanish explorer in 1565, has old streets that recall its Spanish past, while the Historic Area of Colonial Williamsburg, Virginia, is a loving reconstruction of how the heart of this early settlement once looked when it was the capital of Virginia Colony in the 18th century. However, the most striking of all the country's human landmarks are its great cities, with their dazzling skyscrapers, imposing memorials, and elegant public or historic buildings, while American architects, such as Frank Lloyd Wright, have influenced building around the world.

The United States has massive natural resources, including fertile soils, great forests, and deposits of minerals and fossil fuels, including abundant coal, oil, and natural gas. It has exploited these

OPPOSITE TOP
Lincoln Memorial, Washington D.C.

OPPOSITE BELOW
Landscape with cattle, Oregon.

TOP LEFT
Paddle steamer on the Mississippi, Louisiana.

ABOVE
The bright lights of Las Vegas, Nevada.

The United States of America

The United States is the world's fourth largest country. Only Russia, Canada, and China have larger areas. By population, the United States ranks third after China and India.

Area: 3,679,192 sq. miles (9,529,063 sq. km.).
Population (1995): 262,755,260. *Urban:* 74%; *rural:* 26%.
Capital: Washington, D.C.
Largest cities (1990 census): New York City (7,322,564), Los Angeles (3,485,557), Chicago (2,783,728), Houston (629,902), Philadelphia (1,585,577), San Diego (1,110,554), Detroit (1,027,974), Dallas (1,007,618).
Motto: In God We Trust.
National anthem: "The Star-Spangled Banner."
National symbols: *Flower:* rose; *bird:* bald eagle.
Highest point: Mount McKinley, Alaska, 20,320 ft. (6,194 m.).
Lowest point on land: Death Valley, California, 282 ft. (86 m.) below sea level.
Longest river: Missouri, 2,540 miles (4,090 km.).
Largest lake entirely within the United States: Lake Michigan, 22,300 sq. miles (57,757 sq. km.).
Largest island: Hawaii, the "Big Island," in the state of Hawaii, with an area of 4,038 sq. miles (10,458 sq. km.).
Highest recorded temperature: 134°F (57°C), Death Valley recorded in July, 1913.
Lowest recorded temperature: -80°F (-62°C), near Barrow, Alaska, recorded in January 1971.
Wettest place: Mount Waialeale, Kauai, in the state of Hawaii, where it rains up to 350 days every year. The average yearly rainfall is 460 inches (11,684 mm.).

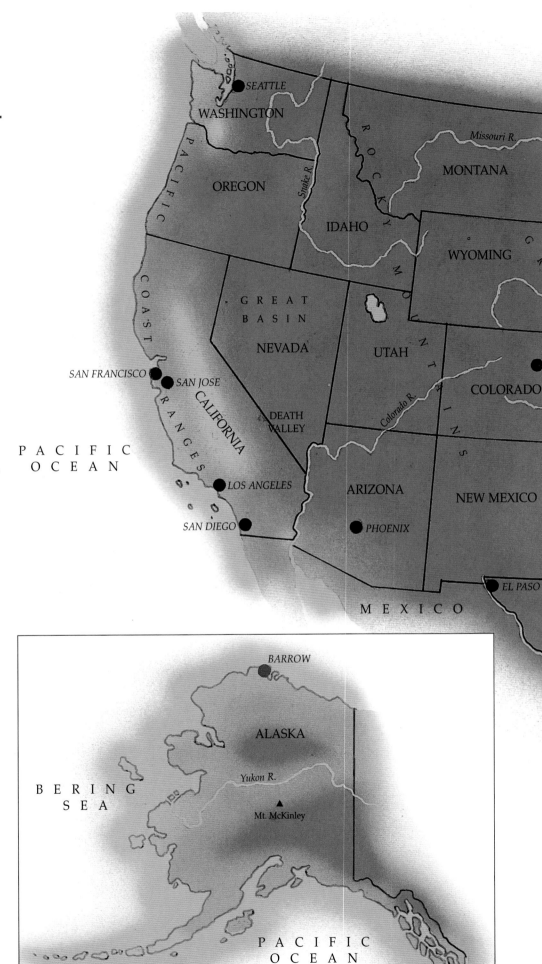

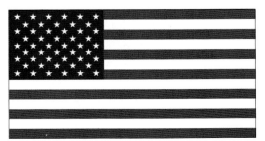

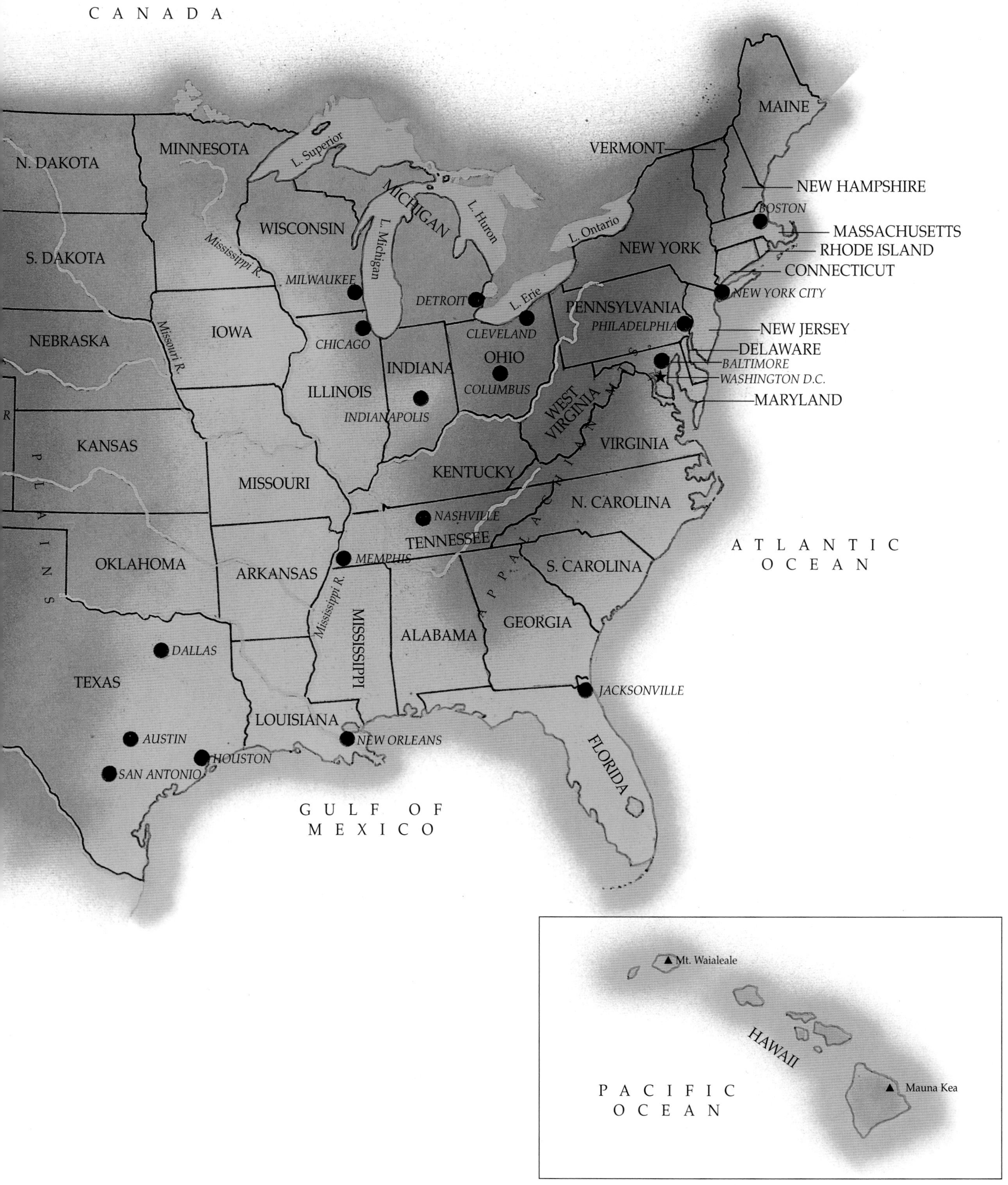

CANADA

N. DAKOTA

MINNESOTA

L. Superior

MAINE

VERMONT

NEW HAMPSHIRE

MICHIGAN

L. Huron

BOSTON

WISCONSIN

L. Michigan

S. DAKOTA

MASSACHUSETTS

L. Ontario

RHODE ISLAND

Mississippi R.

NEW YORK

MILWAUKEE

CONNECTICUT

Missouri R.

DETROIT

L. Erie

NEW YORK CITY

NEBRASKA

IOWA

PENNSYLVANIA

CHICAGO

CLEVELAND

PHILADELPHIA

NEW JERSEY

INDIANA

OHIO

DELAWARE

R

ILLINOIS

COLUMBUS

BALTIMORE

WASHINGTON D.C.

KANSAS

INDIANAPOLIS

WEST VIRGINIA

MARYLAND

VIRGINIA

MISSOURI

KENTUCKY

P

L

A

I

N

S

N. CAROLINA

NASHVILLE

ATLANTIC OCEAN

OKLAHOMA

ARKANSAS

TENNESSEE

MEMPHIS

S. CAROLINA

A

P

P

A

L

A

C

H

I

A

N

S

Mississippi R.

MISSISSIPPI

GEORGIA

DALLAS

ALABAMA

TEXAS

LOUISIANA

JACKSONVILLE

AUSTIN

HOUSTON

NEW ORLEANS

SAN ANTONIO

FLORIDA

GULF OF MEXICO

Mt. Waialeale

HAWAII

PACIFIC OCEAN

Mauna Kea

9

Eastern and Southern States

The Eastern and Southern States include the six New England states, the three Middle Atlantic states, the 14 Southern states, plus Texas and Oklahoma in the southwest. Also included in this section is the nation's capital, Washington, D.C.

This region is steeped in history. It includes St. Augustine, Florida, which was founded by the Spanish in 1565, making it the first permanent European settlement in America. In 1607, Jamestown, Virginia, became the site of the first permanent English settlement, while, in 1620, the Puritans founded the second permanent English settlement in what is now Massachusetts.

The original 13 colonies, which formed the nucleus of the United States following the Revolutionary War of 1775-1783, stretched from Maine, in New England, to Georgia in the South. New England is noted for its scenery, especially in the fall, when its mixed forests are a symphony of color. The Appalachian Mountains extend from Maine, through New England and the Middle Atlantic States, to Alabama. Among the many ranges in the Appalachians are the Great Smoky Mountains, one of the country's most popular national parks, together with the scenic Blue Ridge Parkway in North Carolina and Virginia.

The Southern States contain many battlefields, gracious mansions, and other sites that recall the Old South and the Civil War. In the southwest, the land merges into the open vistas of the West. Here is one of the country's most famous historic sites, the Alamo in Texas.

The Eastern and Southern States have their share of great cities, such as Boston in New England; New York City, the nation's largest, and Philadelphia in the Middle Atlantic States; Baltimore, Jacksonville, Memphis, and Nashville in the Southern States; and Houston, Dallas, San Antonio, El Paso, and Austin in Texas. All these cities, together with Washington, D.C., are among the nation's 25 largest.

Jackson Cathedral, New Orleans, Louisiana.

River-front houses in Essex, Connecticut.

MAINE

VERMONT

NEW HAMPSHIRE

L. Superior

L. Huron

L. Michigan

L. Ontario

MASSACHUSETTES

RHODE ISLAND

NEW YORK

CONNECTICUT

L. Erie

PENNSYLVANIA

NEW JERSEY

DELAWARE

BALTIMORE

WASHINGTON D.C.

MARYLAND

WEST VIRGINIA

VIRGINIA

KENTUCKY

N. CAROLINA

A T L A N T I C
O C E A N

TENNESSEE

OKLAHOMA

ARKANSAS

S. CAROLINA

MISSISSIPPI

ALABAMA

GEORGIA

TEXAS

LOUISIANA

NEW ORLEANS

FLORIDA

SLOPPY JOE'S BAR

*Duval Street,
Key West, Florida.*

Alabama

Alabama, one of the Southern States and nicknamed the "Heart of Dixie," has many associations with the Confederacy. It is the 29th largest state and ranks 22nd in population.

Area: 51,705 sq. miles (133,915 sq.km.).
Population (1995): 4,252,982. *Urban:* 60%; *rural:* 40%.
Capital: Montgomery.
Largest cities (1990 census): Birmingham (265,347), Mobile (196,263), Montgomery (187,543), Huntsville (159,880), Tuscaloosa (77,866).
State motto: *Audemus Jura Nostra Defendere* (We dare defend our rights).
State song: "Alabama."
State symbols: *Flower:* camellia; *bird:* yellowhammer; *tree:* southern pine.
Land features: The Gulf Coast plains make up the southern two-thirds of the state, apart from a hilly strip of prairie called the Black Belt. The north contains the southernmost part of the Appalachian range, including parts of the Cumberland and Piedmont plateaus. The highest point is Cheaha Mountain, at 2,407 ft. (734 m.). The longest rivers, the Alabama and Tombigbee, join not far north of Mobile.
Climate: Alabama has mild winters, though the north is cooler than the south. Summers are hot and the average yearly rainfall ranges from more than 50 inches (1270 mm.) in the north to 65 inches (1651 mm.) on the coast.
Economy: Some coal, oil, natural gas, and limestone are mined and forests cover nearly two-thirds of the land, but the most valuable activity is manufacturing. Manufactures include chemicals, clothing, electronics, metals, pulp and paper, and textiles. Livestock include beef cattle and broiler chickens, while major crops include corn, cotton, hay, peanuts, sorghum, soybeans, tobacco, and wheat. Service industries account for 70% of the state's gross product.
Major attractions: First White House of the Confederacy, Montgomery; George Washington Carver Museum, Tuskegee University; Horseshoe Bend National Military Park, northeast of Lake Martin; U.S. Space and Rocket Center, Huntsville; U.S.S. *Alabama* Memorial Park, Mobile; Vulcan Park, Birmingham.
Famous Alabamians: Nat King Cole, Helen A. Keller, William C. Handy, Joe Louis, Jesse Owens, George Wallace.

KEY DATES

1519   Spanish navigators reached Mobile Bay.
1540   The Spaniard Hernando de Soto explored Alabama.
1702   French Canadians founded Fort Louis on the Mobile River. It became capital of the French colony of Louisiana.
1711   The French moved Fort Louis to the present site of Mobile.
1763   France gave Alabama to Britain.
1783   Britain gave the Mobile area to Spain.
1813   U.S. troops captured Mobile Bay.
1819   Alabama became the 22nd state.
1861   Alabama seceded and became the Republic of Alabama. It joined the Confederacy on February 4 and Montgomery became its first capital.
1868   Alabama was readmitted to the Union.
1950s and 1960s   The civil rights movement was active in the state.
1960   The George C. Marshall Space Flight Center was established at Huntsville.

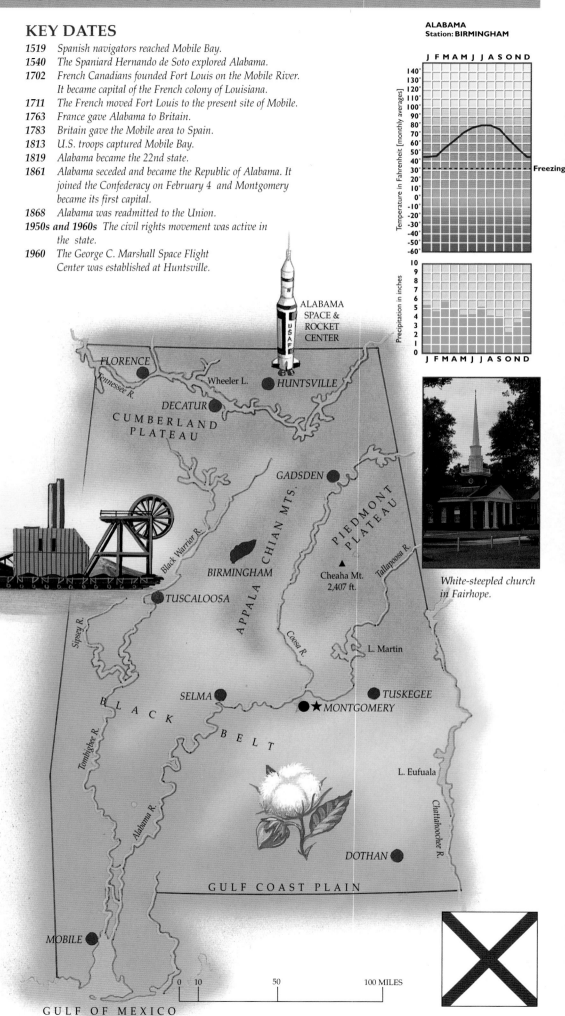

White-steepled church in Fairhope.

Arkansas

Arkansas, one of the Southern States, is nicknamed the *Land of Opportunity*. It is the 29th largest state and it ranks 33rd in population.

Area: 53,187 sq. miles (137,754 sq. km.)
Population (1995): 2,483,769. *Urban:* 52%; *rural:* 48%.
Capital: Little Rock.
Largest cities (1990 census): Little Rock (175,727), Fort Smith (72,798), North Little Rock (61,829, not shown on map), Pine Bluff (57,140), Jonesboro (46,535).
State motto: *Regnat Populus* (The people rule).
State song: "Arkansas."
State symbols: *Flower:* apple blossom; *bird:* mockingbird; *tree:* pine.
Land features: The Mississippi River borders the state in the east and the lowlying Mississippi River plain and the West Gulf coastal plain together make up a sizable part. The main highlands, the Ozark Plateau in the northwest and the Ouachita Mountains in west-central Arkansas, are separated by the Arkansas River valley. The state's highest peak is Magazine Mountain, at 2,753 ft. (839 m.). Forests cover about half of the area.

Climate: The lowlying parts of Arkansas have hot summers and cool winters, though the highlands are cooler than the eastern and southern plains. The state has abundant rainfall and some snow falls on the highlands in winter.

Economy: The chief natural resources include coal, oil, and natural gas, fertile soil and forests of pine and hardwoods. About half of the land is farmed. Broilers and beef cattle are the leading livestock and dairy products are also important. Major crops include soybeans, rice, cotton, and wheat. Processed foods (including animal feed), and electrical equipment are major manufactures. Natural gas is the state's leading mineral product. Service industries account for over six-tenths of the state's gross product.

Major attractions: Crater of Diamonds State Park, in the southwest; Dogpatch U.S.A., an amusement park near Harrison; Eureka Springs in the Ozark Plateau; Fort Smith National Historic Site; Hot Springs National Park; MacArthur Park in Little Rock; and Pea Ridge National Military Park in the northwest.

Famous Arkansans: Hattie Caraway, President Bill Clinton, "Dizzy" Dean, Douglas MacArthur.

KEY DATES

1541 The Spaniard Hernando de Soto explored the area.
1673 French explorers, Father Jacques Marquette and Louis Jolliet, traveled down the Mississippi River.
1682 René-Robert Cavelier, Sieur de la Salle, claimed the Mississippi valley for France; he called the area Louisiana.
1803 The United States bought the Louisiana Territory from France.
1819 The Arkansas Territory was formed from part of the Louisiana Territory.
1836 Arkansas became the 25th state.
1861 Arkansas seceded from the Union.
1868 Arkansas was readmitted to the Union.
1932 Hattie Caraway became the first woman to be elected to the U.S. Senate.
1992 Bill Clinton, former governor of Arkansas, was elected President of the United States.

The Capitol, with monument to Confederate women, Little Rock.

ARKANSAS
Station: LITTLE ROCK

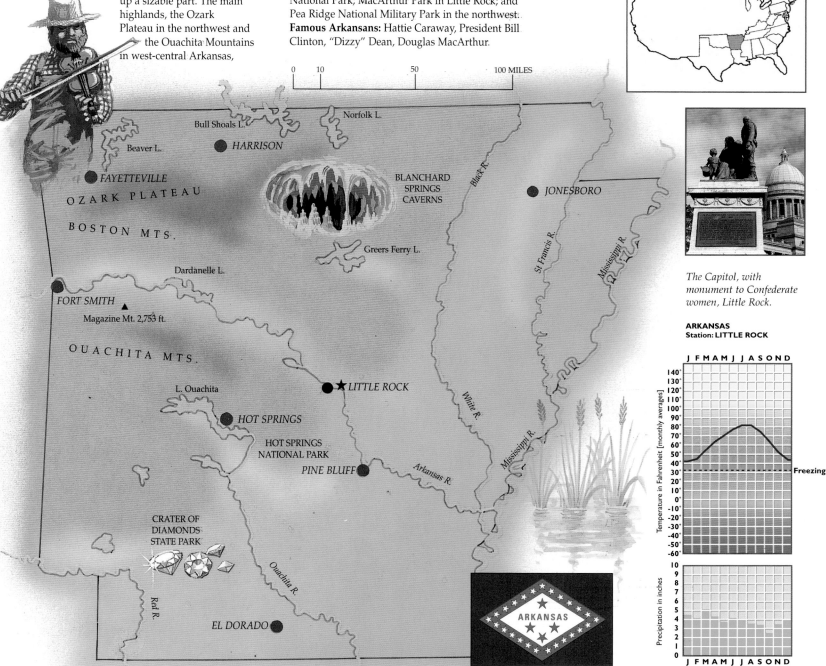

13

Connecticut

Connecticut, one of the six New England states, is nicknamed the Constitution State or the Nutmeg State. It ranks 48th in area and 28th in population.

Area: 5,018 sq. miles (12,997 sq, km,).
Population (1995): 3,274,662. *Urban:* 79%; *rural:* 21%.
Capital: Hartford.
Largest cities (1990 census): Bridgeport (141,686), Hartford (139,739), New Haven (130,474).
State motto: *Qui Transtulit Sustinet* (He who transplanted still sustains).
State song: "Yankee Doodle."
State symbols: *Flower:* mountain laurel; *bird:* robin; *tree:* white oak.
Land features: The narrow coastal lowlands face the Long Island Sound in the south. Inland lie two main upland areas divided by the Connecticut valley lowland that extends north-south from New Haven through Hartford. The state's highest point lies on the its northwest border with Massachusetts. It is a point on the southern slope of Mount Frissell, reaching 2,380 ft. (725 m.) above sea level, though this mountain's highest point is in Massachusetts. The chief waterway is the Connecticut River in the center of the state. Many small lakes and forests cover about 60% of the land.

Climate: Connecticut has cold winters when temperatures fall below freezing and snow is common. Summers are warm and rainfall occurs in every month.
Economy: The state has many manufacturing industries. Transportation equipment is especially important and aircraft engines and parts, helicopters, and submarines are major products. Also important are machinery and computer equipment, electronics and electrical equipment, scientific instruments, and pharmaceuticals. Greenhouse and nursery farming are leading activities, while other farm products include apples, eggs, milk, sweet corn, tobacco, and vegetables. Service industries, notably finance, insurance, and real estate, account for about three-quarters of the state's gross product.
Major attractions: Mark Twain's House, Hartford; Marinelife Aquarium, Mystic; Mystic Seaport; U.S.S. *Nautilus* Memorial, Groton; Whitfield House, Guilford, and other old, attractive colonial buildings in most old towns.
Famous Nutmeggers: Ethan Allen, Phineas Taylor Barnum, Samuel Colt, Nathan Hale, Katherine Hepburn, John Pierpoint Morgan, Harriet Beecher Stowe, Noah Webster.

KEY DATES

1614 The Dutch claimed Connecticut as part of their colony of New Netherland.
1633 Settlers founded the first English settlement in what is now Connecticut.
1636 Hartford, Wethersfield, and Windsor formed the English Connecticut Colony.
1662 England granted a charter to Connecticut Colony.
1776 Connecticut passed a resolution favoring independence.
1788 Connecticut became the 5th state.
1954 Nautilus, the first nuclear powered submarine, was built and launched in Groton.
1979 Connecticut, pursuing anti-pollution policies, passed a law prohibiting the building of nuclear power plants beyond the three existing ones.

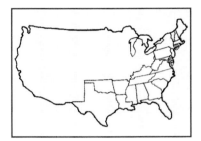

River-front houses, Essex.

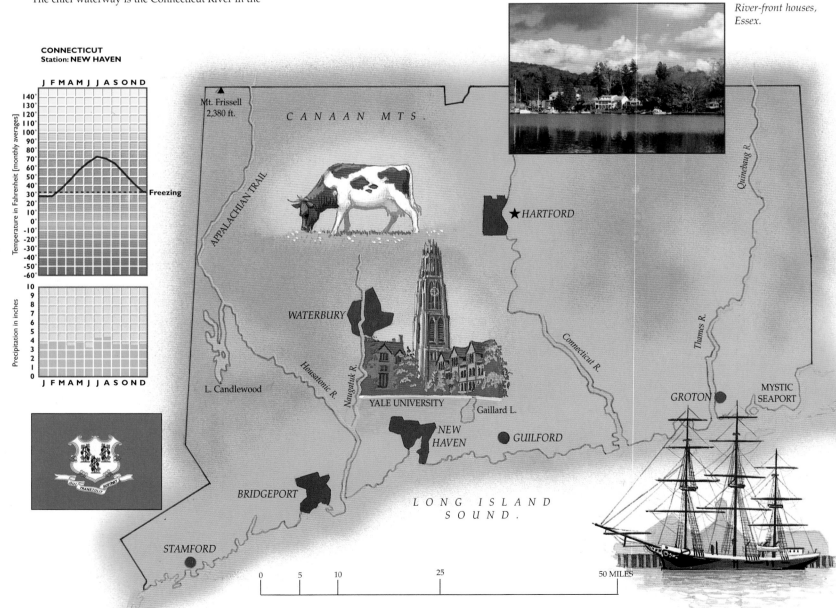

CONNECTICUT
Station: NEW HAVEN

Washington, D.C.

Washington D.C. is the national capital of the United States and the seat of the federal government.

Area: 69 sq. miles (179 sq. km.).
Population (1995): 554,256.
Motto: *Justitia Omnibus* (Justice for all).
Symbols: *Flower:* American beauty rose; *bird:* wood thrush; *tree:* scarlet oak.
Land features: Washington D.C. lies at the meeting point between the Potomac and Anacostia rivers between Virginia and Maryland. The highest point is 410 ft. (125 m.).
Climate: Washington D.C. has hot summers and mild winters, though cold spells sometimes occur. The average precipitation, including rain and melted snow, is 42 inches (1067 mm.). It occurs throughout the year,
Economy: Government services and the tourist industry are the main sources of employment in Washington D.C.
Major attractions: Government buildings and memorials include the United States Capitol and the Library of Congress Supreme Court Building, the White House, the Jefferson Memorial, the Lincoln Memorial, and the Washington Monument. Other attractions include the Arlington National Cemetery, on the west bank of the Potomac River; Ford's Theater and Frederick Douglass National Historic Sites; John F. Kennedy Center for the Performing Arts and national memorial; Smithsonian museums.

1. KENNEDY CENTER
2. WHITE HOUSE
3. LINCOLN MEMORIAL
4. WASHINGTON MONUMENT
5. CAPITOL
6. JEFFERSON MEMORIAL
7. WASHINGTON CATHEDRAL

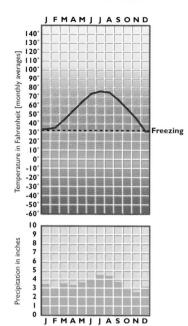

DISTRICT OF COLUMBIA
Station: WASHINGTON D.C.

Capitol Building, Washington D.C.

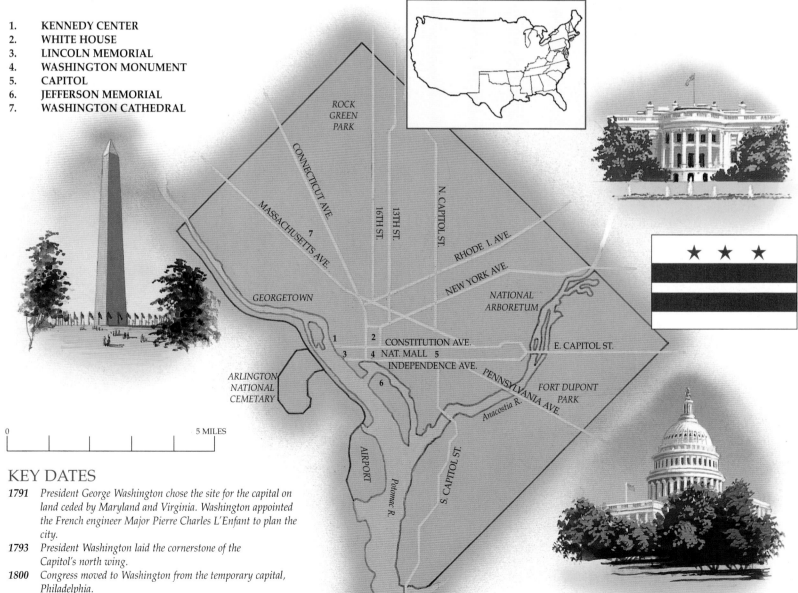

KEY DATES

1791 President George Washington chose the site for the capital on land ceded by Maryland and Virginia. Washington appointed the French engineer Major Pierre Charles L'Enfant to plan the city.
1793 President Washington laid the cornerstone of the Capitol's north wing.
1800 Congress moved to Washington from the temporary capital, Philadelphia.
1802 The city of Washington was incorporated.
1874 The District of Columbia was created, incorporating Washington, Georgetown, and Washington County.

Delaware

Delaware, one of the Southern States, is nicknamed the First State because it was the first to approve the U.S. Constitution on December 7, 1787. It is the second smallest state, but ranks 46th in population.

Area: 2,045 sq. miles (5,294 sq. km.).
Population (1995): 717,197. *Urban:* 71%; *rural:* 29%.
Capital: Dover.
Largest cities (1990 census): Wilmington (71,529), Dover (27,630), Newark (26,463).
State motto: Liberty and Independence.
State song: "Our Delaware."
State symbols: *Flower:* peach blossom; *bird:* blue hen chicken; *tree:* American holly.
Land features: Much of the land in Delaware is flat. The highest region, called the Piedmont, is in the far north. The state's highest point, at 442 ft. (135 m.) above sea level, lies close to the northern border with Pennsylvania. The state lies west of Delaware Bay and the Delaware River, its most important waterway. Forests cover about a third of the land.
Climate: Summers in Delaware are hot, though cool sea breezes bring relief to vacationers on the beaches. Winters are mild but there is usually some snow. Precipitation, including both snow and rain, occurs throughout the year.
Economy: Manufacturing is extremely important to the economy and chemicals, including drugs and plastics, are the leading products. The Wilmington area contains the headquarters of several major chemical companies, including E. I. DuPont de Nemours & Company. Other industries are food processing and the manufacture of automobiles. Farmland covers about half of the state. Livestock raising is the leading type of farming and broiler chickens, milk, and hogs are major products. Crops include apples, barley, corn, soybeans, vegetables, and wheat. Greenhouse and nursery farming are also important, as is fishing. However, service industries, including finance, insurance, and real estate, make up around two-thirds of the state's gross product.
Major attractions: Fort Delaware on Pea Patch Island; Great Cypress Swamp, near Laurel; Henry Francis DuPont Winterthur Museum, near Wilmington; State House, Dover; Zwaanendael Museum, at Lewes.
Famous Delawareans: Thomas F. Bayard, John P. Marquand, Howard Pyle, Caesar Rodney.

KEY DATES

1609 The English explorer Henry Hudson entered Delaware Bay.
1631 The Dutch founded Zwaanendael, near what is now Lewes at the mouth of Delaware Bay.
1638 Swedish settlers founded a colony called New Sweden and set up the area's first permanent European settlement near Wilmington.
1665 The Dutch made New Sweden part of their colony, New Netherland.
1664 The English captured New Netherland.
1776 The "Three Lower Counties," as Delaware was then known, voted for independence from England.
1787 Delaware became the first state of the Union.
1861-65 Delaware fought on the Union side in the Civil War.
1951 The opening of the Delaware Memorial Bridge, linking Delaware and New Jersey, led to an expansion of the state's economy.

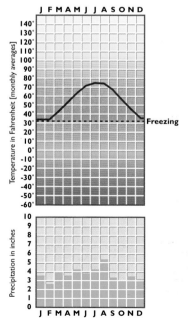

DELAWARE
Station: WILMINGTON

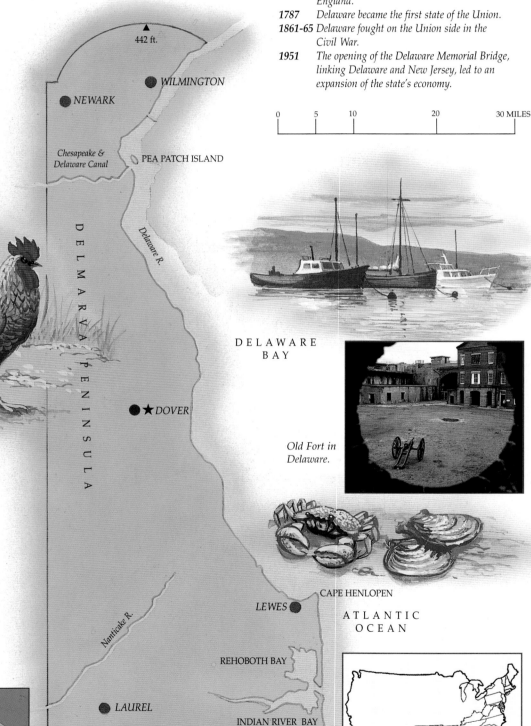

Old Fort in Delaware.

DELAWARE BAY

ATLANTIC OCEAN

Florida

Florida, a Southern State, is called the Sunshine State, because it attracts visitors all the year round and many older people settle there when they retire. The state is the 22nd largest in area, but ranks 4th in population.

Area: 58,664 sq. miles (151,939 sq. km.).
Population (1995): 14,165,570. *Urban:* 84%; *rural:* 16%.
Capital: Tallahassee.
Largest cities (1990 census): Jacksonville (635,230), Miami (358,648), Tampa (280,015), St. Petersburg (240,318), Hialeah (close to Miami and not shown on the map, 164,674), Orlando (164,674), Fort Lauderdale (149,238), Tallahassee (124,773).
State motto: In God We Trust.
State song: "Old Folks at Home" ("Swanee River").
State symbols: *Flower:* orange blossom; *bird:* mockingbird; *tree:* sabal palm.
Land features: The land consists of flat coastal plains with low uplands in the north and center. The highest point, in the northwest, is only 345 ft. (105 m.) above sea level. In the south are areas often covered by water, including the Everglades. The St. Johns River, the state's largest, reaches the sea near Jacksonville. Much of the coast is lined by sand bars, barrier islands and coral reefs. A chain of small islands, called the Florida Keys, extends southwestwards from the southern tip of the state.
Climate: Florida has a warm, moist climate, with mild winters and hot summers, though sea breezes cool coastal areas in summer. The state lies in the path of hurricanes which form in the Atlantic Ocean and sometimes strike the eastern seaboard with tremendous force.
Economy: Service industries (including tourism and the provision of services to retired people) account for around four-fifths of the state's gross product. Manufacturing, especially food processing, is also important as is the manufacture of electrical equipment. Crop growing is another leading activity. Major crops include oranges and other citrus fruits, vegetables (including tomatoes), and sugar cane.
Major attractions: Biscayne National Park; Cypress Gardens, east of Tampa; Everglades National Park; St. Augustine, the oldest permanent European settlement in the United States; Spaceport U.S.A., Cape Canaveral; Walt Disney World which includes Magic Kingdom ® Park, Epcot® and Disney-MGM Studios, Orlando.

Famous Floridians: James Weldon Johnson, Edmund Kirby Smith, Joseph Warren Stilwell.

KEY DATES

1513   The Spaniard, Juan Ponce de León, claimed the area for Spain.
1565   Spanish forces settled St. Augustine after destroying a French Huguenot colony.
1763   Spain gave Florida to England in exchange for Cuba.
1783   Spain regained control of Florida.
1821   Florida came under the control of the U.S.
1861   Florida seceded from the Union and later joined the Confederacy.
1868   Florida was readmitted to the Union.
1958   The first U.S. earth satellite, Explorer I, was launched from Cape Canaveral.
1968   Apollo II was launched from Cape Canaveral, then called Cape Kennedy, putting the first men on the Moon.
1971   Walt Disney World was opened near Orlando.

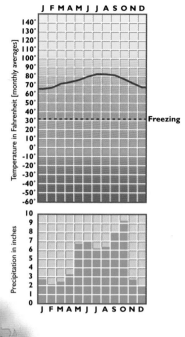

FLORIDA
Station: MIAMI

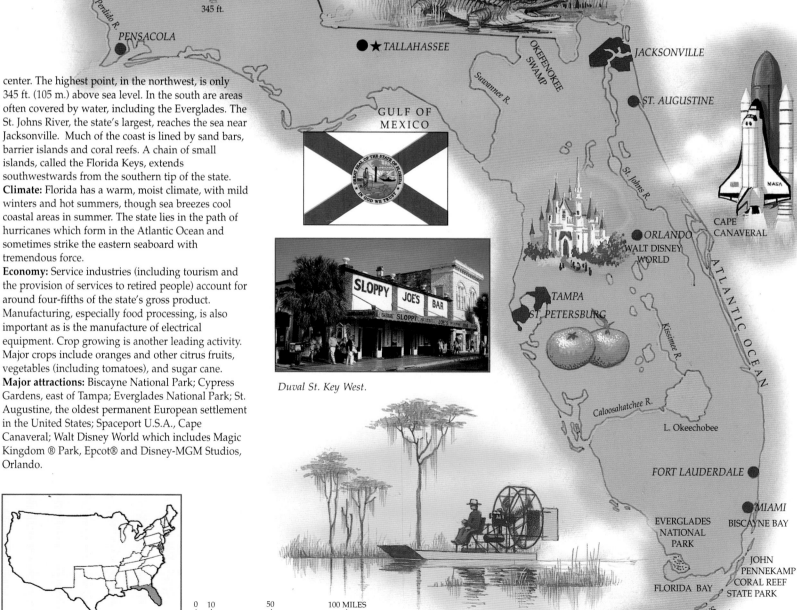

Duval St. Key West.

Goodland waterfront, Marco Island, Florida.

Georgia

Georgia is nicknamed the Empire State of the South, partly because it is the largest state east of the Mississippi River, and partly because of its economic importance. One of the Southern States, it ranks 21st in area and 10th in population.

Area: 58,664 sq. miles (151,939 sq. km.).
Population (1995): 7,200,882. Urban: 62%; rural: 38%.
Capital: Atlanta.
Largest cities (1990 census): Atlanta (393,929), Columbus (178,681), Savannah (137,812), Macon (107,365), Albany (78,804).
State motto: Wisdom, Justice, and Moderation.
State song: "Georgia on My Mind."
State symbols: *Flower*: Cherokee rose; *bird*: brown thrasher; *tree*: live oak.
Land features: Southern Georgia, which faces the Atlantic Ocean, is generally flat, with Okefenokee Swamp in the southeast. To the north, the land rises to the Piedmont, Plateau, a hilly region. The southern boundary of the Piedmont is called the Fall Line, because here the rivers descend in a series of falls and rapids. Parts of the Appalachian Mountains, including a range called the Blue Ridge, make up northern Georgia. This region contains Brasstown Bald Mountain, the state's highest point at 4,784 ft. (1,458 m.) above sea level. Major rivers include the Altamaha, Chattahoochee, Flint and Savannah. Forests cover nearly two-thirds of the land.

Climate: Winters in southern Georgia are mild and summers are hot and humid. But the Appalachian Mountains are cooler and winters are cold. The average yearly rainfall is around 50 inches (1270 mm.).
Economy: Georgia's economy has developed quickly since the 1950s. Leading products include transportation equipment, textiles, processed foods, and paper products. About a third of the land is farmed and the raising of broilers, beef cattle, and hogs is important, while milk is a major product. Cotton was once the leading crop, but it has been overtaken in importance by peanuts, tobacco, soybeans, and corn. Service industries, especially wholesale and retail trades, account for nearly three-quarters of the state's gross product.

Major attractions: Chattahoochee River National Recreation Area; Chickamauga and Chattanooga National Military Park; Cumberland Island National Seashore; Kennesaw Mountain National Battlefield Park near Atlanta; Okefenokee National Wildlife Refuge; sculptures of Confederate leaders at Stone Mountain, near Atlanta.
Famous Georgians: President Jimmy Carter, Ray Charles, John C. Frémont, Joel Chandler Harris, Martin Luther King Jr., Margaret Mitchell, Alice Walker.

KEY DATES

1540	The Spaniard Hernando de Soto traveled through the area.
1732	England granted a charter to establish the Colony of Georgia.
1733	The first English settlers arrived in Georgia.
1788	Georgia became the fourth state of the Union.
1861	Georgia seceded and joined the Confederacy.
1868-70	Georgia was readmitted to the Union in 1868, but was expelled in 1869. However, it was permanently readmitted in 1870.
1977	Jimmy Carter, former Governor of Georgia, became the 39th President of the United States.

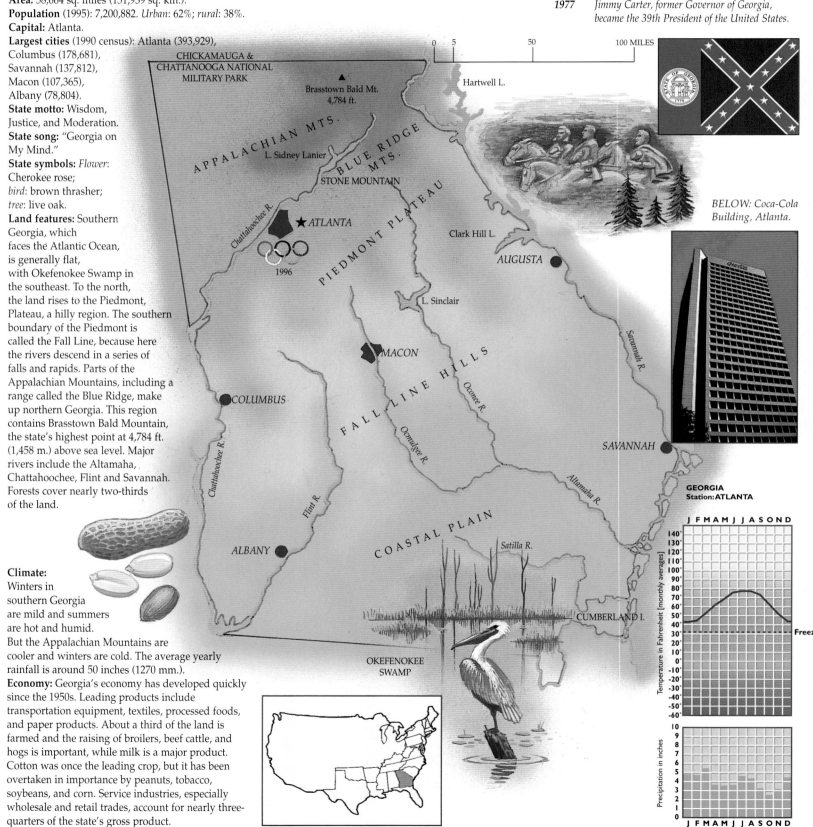

BELOW: Coca-Cola Building, Atlanta.

GEORGIA
Station: ATLANTA

Kentucky

Kentucky, one of the Southern States, is called the Bluegrass State after the blue blossom of the grass that grows around Lexington. It is the 37th largest state, but ranks 24th in population.

Area: 40,410 sq. miles (104,659 sq. km.).
Population (1995): 3,860,219. *Urban:* 51%; *rural:* 49%.
Capital: Frankfort.
Largest cities (1990 census): Louisville (269,555), Lexington (225,366), Owensboro (53,577), Covington (43,646), Bowling Green (41,688), Hopkinsville (29,809), Paducah (27,256), Frankfort (26,535).
State motto: United We Stand, Divided We Fall.
State song: "My Old Kentucky Home."
State symbols: *Flower*: goldenrod; *bird*: Kentucky cardinal; *tree*: Kentucky coffeetree.
Land features: The Cumberland plateau in eastern Kentucky rises to mountain ranges in the southeast, where the state's highest point, Black Mountain, reaches 4,145 ft. (1,263 m.) Most of western Kentucky forms part of the Interior Plains. It includes the Bluegrass Region in north-central Kentucky. Limestone rocks are common in south-central Kentucky and many caves lie beneath the surface. The Ohio River, which forms the state's northern border, flows into the Mississippi River, which forms the boundary in the southwest. Forests cover more than two-fifths of the land.
Climate: Kentucky has warm summers and cool winters. The precipitation is abundant and snow falls on the Appalachian region in the southeast.
Economy: Natural resources include fertile soils and large coalfields. Farmlands cover nearly three-fifths of the land and the raising of beef cattle and thoroughbred horses are leading activities. Milk, hogs, eggs, and broilers are also important. Crops include tobacco, soybeans, corn, and wheat. The main manufacturing industry is food processing and Kentucky is known for its bourbon whiskey. Transportation equipment, machinery, and electrical equipment are other leading products.
Major attractions: Abraham Lincoln Birthplace National Historic Site, south of Louisville; Cumberland Gap National Historical Park, in the southeast; Fort Knox; Kentucky Horse Park, Lexington; Land Between the Lakes, a recreation area in the west; Mammoth Cave National Park.
Famous Kentuckians: Muhammad Ali (Cassius Clay), Kit Carson, Jefferson Davis, President Abraham Lincoln, President Zachary Taylor, Robert Penn Warren.

KEY DATES

1774 *The first permanent white settlement was established at Harrodsburg.*
1775 *Daniel Boone led a group of settlers through the Cumberland Gap into what is now Kentucky,*
1776 *Kentucky became a county of Virginia.*
1792 *Kentucky became the 15th state of the Union.*
1861-5 *Kentucky wanted to remain neutral in the Civil War, but it stayed in the Union.*
1936 *The U.S. Treasury Department completed its gold depository at Fort Knox.*

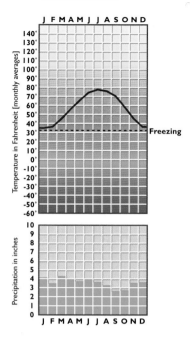

KENTUCKY
Station: LOUISVILLE

Kentucky Derby Museum Gala, Louisville.

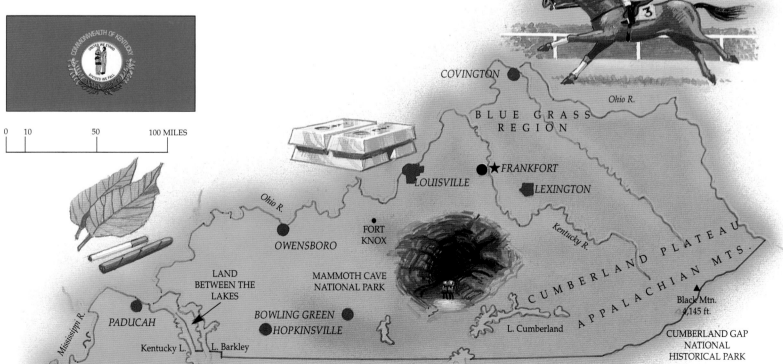

COVINGTON

Ohio R.

BLUE GRASS REGION

★ FRANKFORT

LOUISVILLE

LEXINGTON

Ohio R.

Kentucky R.

FORT KNOX

OWENSBORO

LAND BETWEEN THE LAKES

MAMMOTH CAVE NATIONAL PARK

CUMBERLAND PLATEAU

APPALACHIAN MTS.

Black Mtn. 4,145 ft.

L. Cumberland

CUMBERLAND GAP NATIONAL HISTORICAL PARK

BOWLING GREEN

HOPKINSVILLE

PADUCAH

Mississippi R.

Kentucky L. L. Barkley

0 10   50   100 MILES

21

Louisiana

Louisiana, one of the Southern States, is nicknamed the Pelican State for the state bird symbol, namely the brown pelican that was once common along the coast. It is the 31st largest state by area and the 21st in population.

Area: 47,752 sq. miles (123,677 sq. km.).
Population (1995): 4,342,334. *Urban:* 69%; *rural:* 31%.
Capital: Baton Rouge.
Largest cities (1990 census): New Orleans (496,936), Baton Rouge (219,531), Shreveport (198,518), Metairie (close to New Orleans and not shown on the map, 149,428), Lafayette (94,438).
State motto: Union, Justice and Confidence.
State song: "Give Me Louisiana."
State symbols: *Flower:* magnolia; *bird:* brown pelican; *tree:* bald cypress.
Land features: Plains cover most of Louisiana. The chief river, the Mississippi, carries huge amounts of silt into the sea. Some silt is dropped near the river's mouth, and this has created a huge delta, a lowlying region which makes up about a quarter of the state's area. The state's highest point is Driskill Mountain, which reaches 535 ft. (163 m.) in the north. Forests cover about half of the land.
Climate: Louisiana has a hot, humid climate, with plenty of rainfall throughout the year. Hurricanes often strike the state, especially in September. They sometimes cause great damage.
Economy: The state's natural resources include its fertile soils, its forests, and its oil and gas fields. Mining is important in the economy. Oil and gas are the leading products, followed by sulfur and salt. Major industries include the manufacture of chemicals and the processing of oil and coal products. Other manufactures include transportation equipment, paper products, and processed foods. Many farmers grow crops, notably cotton, rice, sugar cane and corn. Also important are beef and dairy cattle raising, together with fishing, especially for shrimp. However, service industries account for nearly two-thirds of the state's gross product.

Major attractions: Acadiana, a region in south-central Louisiana famed for its Cajun culture; Natchitoches, the state's oldest town; New Orleans French Quarter, Dixieland jazz and Mardi Gras; Jean Lafitte National Historical Park and Preserve; Poverty Point National Monument, east of Monroe in the north.
Famous Louisianans: Louis Armstrong, Pierre Beauregard, Van Cliburn, Huey Long, Leonidas K. Polk.

KEY DATES

1541 The Spaniard Hernando de Soto explored the area.
1699 The French colony of Louisiana, which covered a large area in what is now the central United States, was created.
1762 Spain took control of Louisiana.
1800 France again took control of Louisiana.
1803 The United States bought Louisiana from France.
1812 Louisiana became the 18th state of the Union.
1815 In the Battle of New Orleans, Andrew Jackson defeated the British.
1861 Louisiana left the Union and joined the Confederacy in the Civil War.
1868 Louisiana was readmitted to the Union.
1901 Oil was discovered.
1935 Huey Long was assassinated
1992 Hurricane Andrew does great damage in Louisiana.

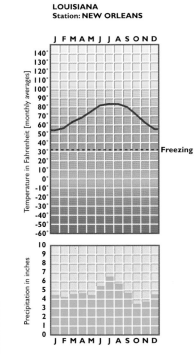

LOUISIANA
Station: NEW ORLEANS

Jackson Cathedral, New Orleans.

Mardi Gras, New Orleans.

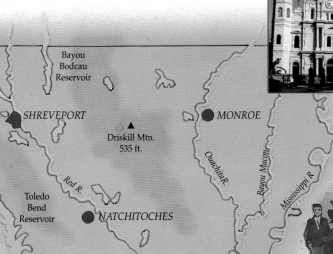

Bayou Bodcau Reservoir

SHREVEPORT

MONROE

Driskill Mtn. 535 ft.

Red R.

Ouachita R.

Bayou Macon

Mississippi R

Toledo Bend Reservoir

NATCHITOCHES

ALEXANDRIA

Sabine R.

★ BATON ROUGE

L. Maurepas

Lake Pontchartrain

Pearl R.

LAKE CHARLES

LAFAYETTE

Grand L.

Sabine L.

Calcasieu L.

Grand L.

White L.

L. Salvador

NEW ORLEANS

BRETON SOUND

CHANDELEU ISLANDS

MARSH I.

GULF OF MEXICO

MISSISSIPPI DELTA

UNION, JUSTICE & CONFIDENCE

Maine

Maine, in New England, is nicknamed the Pine Tree State after the trees that once covered most of the land. It is the 39th largest state by area and the 39th in population.

Area: 33,265 sq. miles (86,156 sq. km.).
Population (1995): 1,241,382. *Urban:* 52%; *rural:* 48%.
Capital: Augusta (population 1990 census, 21, 325).
Largest cities (1990 census): Portland (64,358), Lewiston (39,757), Bangor (33,181).
State motto: *Dirigo* (I direct).
State song: "State of Maine Song."
State symbols: *Flower:* white pine cone and tassel; *bird:* chickadee; *tree:* white pine.
Land features: Dotted along the coast are thousands of small islands. The largest, Mount Desert, is part of Acadia National Park. Inland lie the coastal lowlands, which rise to uplands, with the White Mountains in the west. Maine's highest peak is Mount Katahdin, which reaches 5,268 ft. (1,606 m.) in the center of the state. Maine has more than 2,500 lakes and ponds and more than 5,000 rivers and streams. Forests cover about nine-tenths of the land.
Climate: Marine; has a cool climate and the coast is chilled by winds that blow across the Labrador Current, a cold current that flows from the Arctic. Summers are mild, but winters are cold. In winter, the precipitation takes the form of snow, which increases inland.
Economy: Maine's natural resources include forests and fertile soils. The forests supply the lumber used for the leading industry, the manufacture of paper products. Other leading manufactures are electrical equipment, transportation equipment, and other wood products. Farmland covers only about 7% of the state. Livestock rearing is important and milk and eggs are leading products. Major crops include potatoes, oats, and hay, grown for animal feed. Apples are the leading fruit. However, service industries account for seven-tenths of the state's gross product.
Major attractions: Acadia National Park; Bar Harbor, Mount Desert Island; Penobscot Marine Museum, Searsport; Wadsworth-Longfellow House, Portland; St. Croix Island International Historic Site in the southeast.
Famous Down Easters: Hannibal Hamlin, Stephen King, Henry Wadsworth Longfellow, Sir Hiram and Hudson Maxim, Edna St. Vincent Millay, Margaret Chase Smith.

KEY DATES

1000 *Vikings may have visited the coast of what is now Maine.*
1498 *An Italian, John Cabot, probably explored the Maine coast.*
1607 *English settlers founded a colony at the mouth of the Kennebec River.*
1691 *Maine became part of Massachusetts.*
1775 *The first sea battle of the Revolutionary War took place off the Maine coast.*
1820 *Maine became the 23rd state.*
1940s *Margaret Chase Smith became the first women in the United States to serve in both houses of Congress.*

0   10   50   100 MILES

MAINE
Station: PORTLAND

Chamberlain L.

Chesuncook L. ▲

Mt. Katahdin
5,268 ft.

Permadumcook L.

Moosehead L.

Flagstaff L.

Rangeley Lakes

Kennebec R.

Penobscot R.

St. John R.

St. Croix R.

WHITE MOUNTAINS

● ★ BANGOR

SEARSPORT ●

Androscoggin R.

● AUGUSTA

● LEWISTON

Sebago L.

● PORTLAND

MT. DESERT ISLAND
ACADIA NATIONAL PARK

ATLANTIC OCEAN

BELOW: Autumn scene, Maine.

Maryland

Maryland was nicknamed the Old Line State after the "troops of the line," who fought in the Revolutionary War. One of the Southern States, it ranks 42nd in area, but 19th in population.

Area: 10,460 sq. miles (27,091 sq. km.).
Population (1995): 5,042,438. *Urban:* 80%; *rural:* 20%.
Capital: Annapolis (population 1990 census 33,195).
Largest cities (1990 census): Baltimore (736,014), Silver Spring (76,046), Columbia (75,883).
State motto: *Fatti Maschii, Parole Femine* (Manly Deeds, Womanly Words).
State song: "Maryland, My Maryland."
State symbols: *Flower:* black-eyed Susan; *bird:* Baltimore auriole; *tree:* white oak.
Land features: Coastal plains surround Chesapeake Bay in the east. To the west, the land rises to a region called the Piedmont Plateau and then to the ranges and plateaus of the Appalachian Mountains. The highest point, in the far west, is Backbone Mountain, which reaches 3,360 ft. (1,024 m.). Most of the state's rivers, including the Potomac which forms the southern and southwestern boundary, flow into Chesapeake Bay. Forests cover about two-fifths of the land.
Climate: Summers are hot and winters mild in Maryland, though the mountains in the

from Cumberland to Washington, D.C.; Edgar Allan Poe House, Baltimore; Fort McHenry National Monument and Shrine, Baltimore; St. Mary's City, Maryland's first colonial settlement,west of Lexington Park; U.S. Naval Academy, Annapolis.
Famous Marylanders: Benjamin Banneker, Francis Scott Key, Babe Ruth, Upton Sinclair.

KEY DATES

1608 The English Captain John Smith explored Chesapeake Bay.
1634 The first settlers reached Maryland. They founded St. Mary's City, near the southern tip of the western shore.
1776 Maryland declared its independence from England.
1788 Maryland became the seventh state of the Union.
1791 Land was set aside for the District of Columbia.
1812 Several battles of the 1812 War were fought in Maryland.
1862 The battle of Antietam was fought during the Civil War.
1864 Maryland adopted an antislavery constitution.
1952 The Chesapeake Bay Bridge was opened.

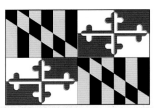

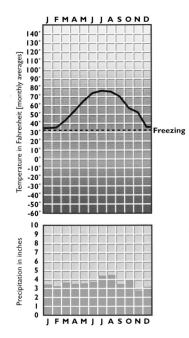

northwest are cooler than the Atlantic coast regions. The rainfall is plentiful throughout the year. Snow falls in winter, especially in the northwest.
Economy: Maryland has fertile soils and farmland covers about a third of the state. Livestock farming is important and major products include broiler chickens and milk. Greenhouse and nursery products, including flowers and ornamental shrubs, are important, while the leading crops are soybeans, tobacco, and corn. Vegetables (including tomatoes) and fruits, notably apples, are also grown. Maryland is also one of the leading states in producing clams and oysters. However, service industries account for more than four-fifths of the state's gross product. The chief service industries are community, social, and personal services, including health care.
Major attractions: Antietam National Battlefield in north-central Maryland; Chesapeake and Ohio Canal, which runs

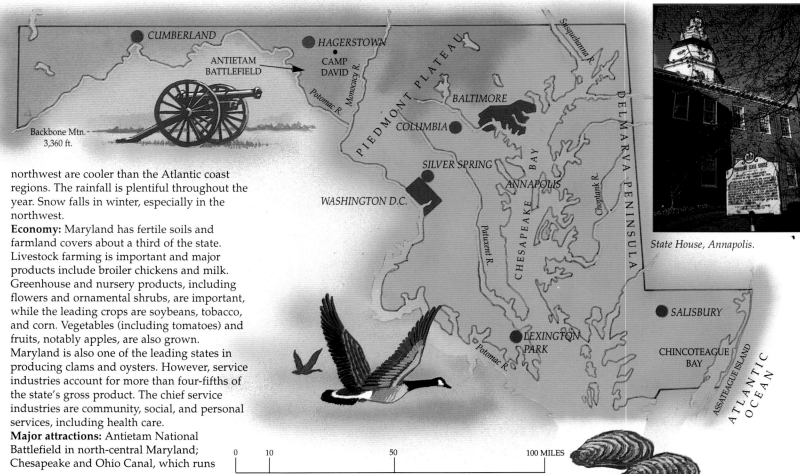

State House, Annapolis.

Massachusetts

Massachusetts, in New England, is nicknamed the Bay State after Massachusetts Bay where the Puritans founded their colony. It is the 45th largest state, though it ranks 13th in population.

Area: 8,284 sq. miles (21,455 sq. km.).
Population (1995): 6,073,550. *Urban:* 84%; *rural:* 16%.
Capital: Boston.
Largest cities (1990 census): Boston (574,283), Worcester (169,759), Springfield (156,983), Lowell (103,439), New Bedford (99,922).
State motto: *Ense Petit Placidam Sub Libertate Quietem* (By the sword we seek peace, but peace only under liberty).
State song: "All Hail to Massachusetts."
State symbols: *Flower:* mayflower; *bird:* chickadee; *tree:* American elm.
Land features: Eastern Massachusetts is a lowlying plain. It includes Nantucket Island and Martha's Vineyard, together with several small islands. Moraine (soil and rock dumped by ice sheets at the end of the Ice Age) covers much of the land. To the east is an upland area divided into two parts by the Connecticut River. But the highest peaks are in the far west. They include Mount Greylock, the state's highest point at 3,491 ft. (1,064 m.) in the northwest. Forests cover about three-fifths of the land.
Climate: The state has cold, snowy winters and warm summers, though temperatures are lower in the western uplands. Hurricanes sometimes strike the area.
Economy: Massachusetts has fertile soils and farmland covers

Historical Park; Plymouth Rock, Plymouth Plantation and Mayflower II, Plymouth; Provincetown artists' colony; Salem; Walden Pond, near Concord, northwest of Boston.
Famous Bay Staters: Presidents John Adams and John Quincy Adams, Samuel Adams, President George Bush, Emily Dickinson, Ralph Waldo Emerson, Nathaniel Hawthorne, Oliver Wendell Holmes, President John F. Kennedy, Samuel Morse, Edgar Allan Poe, Paul Revere, Henry David Thoreau, James McNeill Whistler.

KEY DATES

1000   *Leif Ericson, a Norse explorer, may have reached what is now Massachusetts.*
1620   *Sailing from England, the Pilgrims reached the area.*
1630   *Boston was founded by Puritans.*
1770   *British soldiers killed several people in the Boston Massacre.*
1773   *The Boston Tea Party took place as a protest against British taxation.*
1775   *The American Revolution began at Concord and Lexington.*
1788   *Massachusetts became the sixth state of the Union.*
1959   *The U.S. Navy launched Long Beach, the first nuclear surface ship, at Quincy, south of Boston.*

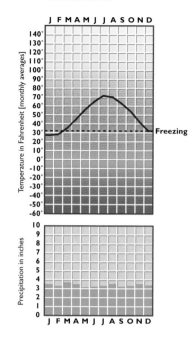

MASSACHUSETTS
Station: BOSTON

LEFT: *Faneuil Hall, Boston.*

over 13% of the state. Greenhouse and nursery products, such as flowers and ornamental plants, are important, while major farm products include cranberries, milk, and hay. Fishing is also important. Manufactures include machinery, (including computers), scientific instruments, and electrical equipment. Tourism is important and service industries account for about 75% of the state's gross product.
Major attractions: Boston's Freedom Trail following historic sites; Cape Cod National Seashore; Harvard University, Cambridge; Minute Man National

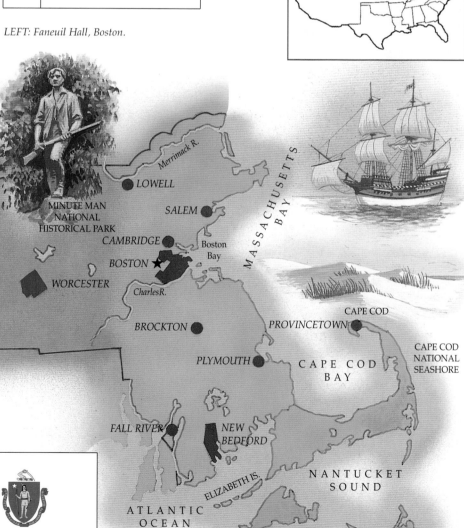

Mississippi

Mississippi, nicknamed the Magnolia State, ranks 31st in area and 31st in population. One of the Southern States, it is rich in reminders of the Old South which existed before the Civil War, though it also has many modern industries.

Area: 47,689 sq. miles (123,514 sq. km.).
Population (1995): 2,697,243. Urban: 53%; rural: 47%.
Capital: Jackson.
Largest cities (1990 census): Jackson (196,637), Biloxi (46,319), Greenville (45,225), Hattiesburg (41,906), Meridian (41,036), Gulfport (40,775).
State motto: *Virtute et Armis* (By valor and arms).
State song: "Go Mississippi."
State symbols: *Flower*: magnolia; *bird*: mockingbird; *tree*: magnolia.
Land features: Plains and low hills make up most of Mississippi. The highest point, Woodall Mountain, reaches 806 ft. (246 m.) in the northeast corner of the state. The Mississippi River forms the western border of the state, and the plain along the river is covered by fertile silt, which was spread over the land during floods. Today, levees (strengthened river banks) prevent dangerous flooding in many areas. Another fertile area, called the Black Belt, extends into eastern Mississippi from Alabama. Forests cover about half of the state.
Climate: The state has long, hot summers and mild winters, with ample rainfall throughout the year. In the south, Mississippi borders the Gulf of Mexico from which hurricanes sometimes arrive, causing great damage.
Economy: Fertile soils, abundant water supplies, and valuable deposits of oil and natural gas are the state's chief natural resources. Farmland covers nearly half of the state. The leading farm animals are broilers and beef and dairy cattle. The most important crops are cotton and soybeans. Corn, grain sorghum, hay, peanuts, rice and wheat are also grown. Manufactures include processed food products, transportation equipment (including ships and automobile parts), electrical equipment, and wood products. However, service industries account for two-thirds of the state's gross product.
Major attractions: Beauvoir, Jefferson Davis's last home, near Woodville; Biloxi, Shrimp Festival in June; Gulf Islands National Seashore; Jackson, Old and New Capitols; Natchez, stately homes; Tupelo, Elvis Presley's birthplace; Vicksburg National Military Park.
Famous Mississippians:
William Faulkner,
Elvis Presley, Leontyne Price,
Eudora Welty,
Tennessee Williams,
Richard Wright.

KEY DATES

1540 The Spanish explorer Hernando de Soto visited the area that is now Mississippi.
1699 A French colony was established at Old Biloxi.
1763 Following the French and Indian War, Mississippi was ruled by England.
1798 The Mississippi Territory was set up.
1817 Mississippi became the 20th state of the Union.
1861 Mississippi seceded from the Union and Mississippi troops served in the Confederate army.
1870 Mississippi was readmitted to the Union.
1939 Oil was discovered in Mississippi.
1960s Civil rights activities occurred and schools were desegregated in 1969.

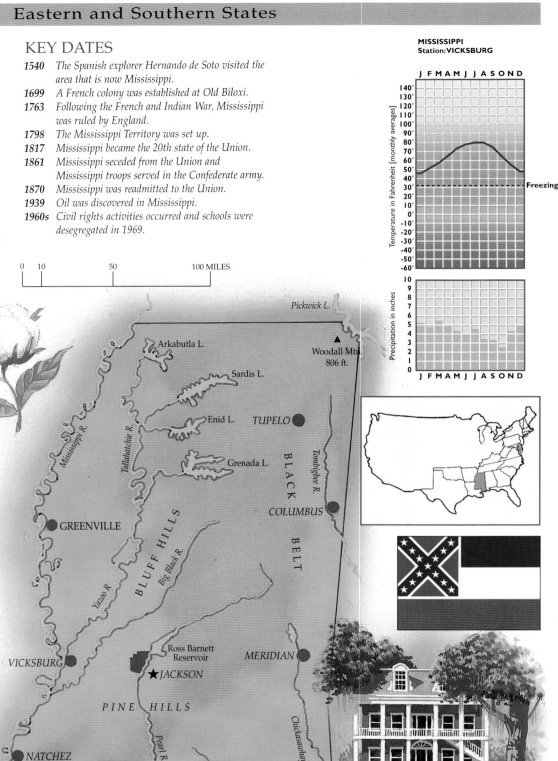

MISSISSIPPI
Station: VICKSBURG

Mississippi River at Natchez, Mississippi.

New Hampshire

NEW HAMPSHIRE
Station: NEWARK

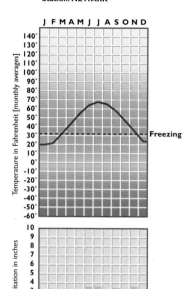

New Hampshire, in New England, was nicknamed the Granite State after its large deposits of this hard rock. It is the 44th largest state and ranks 42nd in population.

Area: 9,279 sq. miles (24,032 sq. km.).
Population (1995): 1,148,253. *Urban:* 52%; *rural:* 48%.
Capital: Concord.
Largest cities (1990 census): Manchester (99,332), Nashua (79,662), Concord (36,006).
State motto: Live Free or Die.
State song: " Old New Hampshire."
State symbols: *Flower:* purple lilac; *bird:* purple finch; *tree:* white birch.
Land features: From a small area of coastal plains in the southeast, the land rises to the New England upland, with the White Mountains in the north. The White Mountains contain New Hampshire's highest peak, Mount Washington, which reaches 6,288 ft. (1,917 m.). One of the state's chief rivers is the Merrimack, which flows south from the White Mountains through Concord into Massachusetts. The Connecticut River, which forms the state's border with Vermont, also flows into Massachusetts. New Hampshire has more than 1,000 lakes and forests which cover about four-fifths of the land.
Climate: New Hampshire has cold, snowy winters and mild summers. The climate on the mountains is sometimes severe, with heavy snowfalls in the north and west. The world's fastest wind speed, 231 m.p.h. (371 km./h.), was recorded on Mount Washington in 1934.
Economy: The state's natural resources include large forests and reserves of granite. Farmland covers about 9% of New Hampshire. Dairy farming is important and hay, which is grown to feed cattle, is the leading crop. Fruit (especially apples), and vegetables are also important. Manufacturing is an important activity. Manufactures include machinery (notably computers), scientific instruments and electrical equipment. Tourism, especially winter sports in the White Mountains, helps to boost the economy and service industries account for two-thirds of the state's gross product.
Major attractions: Lake Winnipesaukee; Mount Washington; Old Man of the Mountain on Profile Mountain; Shaker village, north of Concord; Saint-Gaudens National Historic Site; White Mountain National Forest.
Famous New Hampshirites: Salmon P. Chase, Mary Baker Eddy, Horace Greeley, President Franklin Pierce, Alan B. Shepard Jr., Daniel Webster.

White timber church, Center Harbor.

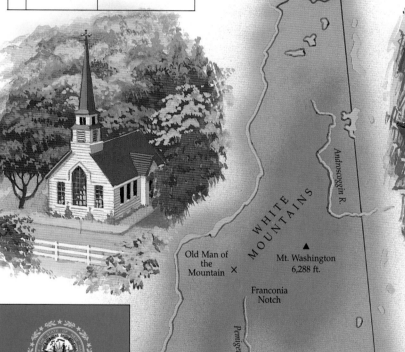

KEY DATES

1603 *An English ship explored the coastal area.*
1641 *New Hampshire became part of Massachusetts Colony.*
1680 *New Hampshire became a separate colony.*
1776 *New Hampshire broke away from Britain and was the first colony to form a government which was completely independent of Britain.*
1788 *New Hampshire became the ninth state of the Union.*
1853 *Franklin Pierce became the 14th President of the United States.*
1961 *New Hampshirite Alan B. Shepard Jr. became the first American in space.*

Squam Lake, New Hampshire. The house featured in the movie On Golden Pond.

New Jersey

New Jersey, one of the Middle Atlantic States, is nicknamed the Garden State for its many truck farms, orchards and flower gardens. It is the 46th largest state, but in population ranks 9th.

Area: 7,787 sq. miles (20,168 sq. km.).
Population (1995): 7,945,298. *Urban:* 89%; *rural:* 11%.
Capital: Trenton.
Largest cities (1990 census): Newark (275,221), Jersey City (228,517), Paterson (140,891).
State motto: Liberty and Prosperity.
State song: None.
State symbols: *Flower:* purple violet; *bird:* eastern goldfinch; *tree:* red oak.
Land features: Southern New Jersey consists of a broad plain bordering the Atlantic Ocean. Much of the coast is bordered by golden beaches, salt marshes, and lagoons. The land rises to the north, which contains the Piedmont Plateau and part of the Appalachian Mountain system. The highest peak, High Point, reaches 1,803 ft. (550 m.) in the far north. The chief rivers are the Delaware, which forms the state's western border and flows into Delaware Bay, and the Hudson, which forms the boundary with New York in the northeast. Forests cover about two-fifths of the land.
Climate: Winters are cold and snowy, especially in the uplands. Summers are hot, though cool sea breezes lower temperatures along the coast. The precipitation, including rain and melted snow, is abundant throughout the state.
Economy: Natural resources include fertile soils and building stone. Greenhouse and nursery farming are important, and major products include flowers and ornamental shrubs. Other farm products include milk, fruits, and vegetables, while corn, hay, and soybeans are major crops. New Jersey is a leading industrial state. Major manufactures include chemicals and chemical products, processed food products, printed materials, transportation equipment, electrical and electronic equipment, and machinery. Tourism is an important activity, especially in the resorts along the coast. Service industries account for more than three-quarters of the state's gross product.
Major attractions: Atlantic City and other seaside resorts; Delaware Water Gap in the northwest; Edison National Historic Site, West Orange, north of Newark; Morristown National Historical Park, which includes George Washington's winter headquarters in 1779-80; Princetown, university and battlefield.
Famous New Jerseyans: Count Basie, President Grover Cleveland, James Fenimore Cooper, Stephen Crane, Paul Robeson, H. Norman Schwarzkopf, Frank Sinatra.

KEY DATES

1524 The Italian explorer Giovanni da Verrazano, sailing for France, reached the New Jersey coast.
1609 Henry Hudson sailed up the Hudson River.
1660 The Dutch founded the first permanent settlement at Bergen, on part of what is now Jersey City.
1664 England took control of the area.
1787 New Jersey became the third state of the Union.
1885 Grover Cleveland was elected 22nd president of the United States.
1893 Grover Cleveland was reelected 24th president of the United States.
1978 Gambling casinos were opened in Atlantic City.

0   10   25   50 MILES

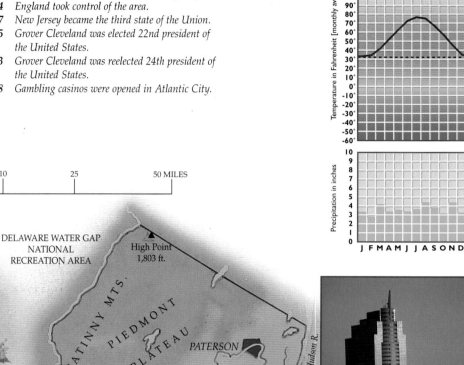

NEW JERSEY
Station: NEWARK

New Jersey viewed across the Hudson from Manhattan.

New York

New York, a Middle Atlantic State, was nicknamed the Empire State possibly because George Washington said that it might become the center of a new empire. It is the 30th largest state, but it ranks 3rd in population.

Area: 52,735 sq. miles (136,583 sq, km.).
Population (1995): 18,136,081. *Urban:* 85%; *rural:* 15%.
Capital: Albany.
Largest cities (1990 census): New York City (7,322,564), Buffalo (328,175), Rochester (230,356), Yonkers (188,082), Syracuse (163,660), Albany (100,031).
State motto: *Excelsior* (Ever upward).
State song: "I Love New York."
State symbols: *Flower:* rose; *bird:* bluebird; *tree:* sugar maple.
Land features: Southern New York, including Long Island, faces the Atlantic Ocean. Inland lie two large uplands, the Allegheny Plateau and the Adirondack Mountains in the north. The Adirondacks have Mount Marcy, the state's highest point at 5,344 ft. (1,629 m.). The main lowlands are the valleys of the Hudson and Mohawk rivers (an important trade route), the plains bordering Lakes Erie and Ontario, and the lowlands bordering the St. Lawrence River in the northwest. Besides the two Great Lakes, the state also has thousands of smaller lakes, while forests cover about half the state.
Climate: Much of New York has hot summers and cold, snowy winters, though the uplands are considerably cooler than the lowlands. The precipitation, including rain and melted snow, is abundant, giving the state ample water supplies.
Economy: New York is a leading business, financial, tourist and transportation center, and service industries account for about four-fifths of the state's gross product. The state ranks second only to California in manufacturing. Manufactures include printed materials, scientific instruments, machinery, chemicals, and electrical equipment. Dairy farming is important and milk is a leading farm product. Beef cattle are raised and crops include corn, fruits, hay, and vegetables. Fishing is another valuable industry.

Major attractions: Finger Lakes National Forest; New York City, its architecture, museums and theaters; Niagara Falls and the Great Lakes; Saratoga National Historical Park, north of Albany; Statue of Liberty National Monument; West Point, north of New York City.
Famous New Yorkers: George Eastman, George and Ira Gershwin, President Millard Fillmore, Julia Ward Howe, Herman Melville, Presidents Franklin Delano Roosevelt, Theodore Roosevelt, and Martin Van Buren and Walt Whitman.

KEY DATES

1609   The explorer Henry Hudson sailed up the Hudson River.
1624   The Dutch founded the first permanent European settlement in the area.
1664   The Dutch surrendered New Amsterdam (New York) to England.
1776   New York declared its support for the Declaration of Independence.
1788   New York became the 11th state of the Union.
1946   New York City became the permanent home of the United Nations.

NEW YORK
Station: NEW YORK CITY

Manhattan Seaport, New York.

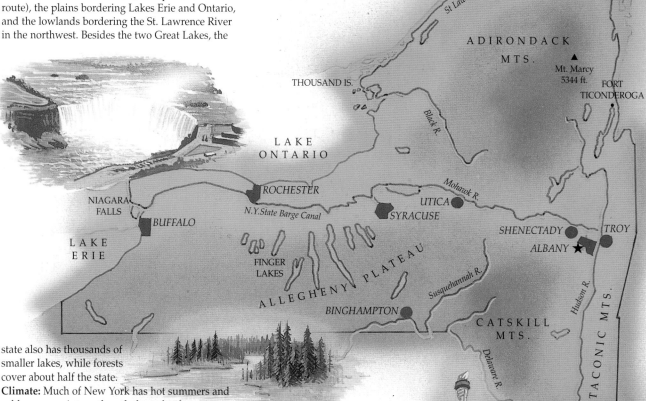

0   10   50   100 MILES

Midtown Manhattan – panorama from the Empire State Building.

North Carolina

North Carolina, nicknamed the Tar Heel State, is one of the Southern States. It is the 28th largest, though it ranks 11th in population.

Area: 52,669 sq. miles (136,412 sq. km.).
Population (1995): 7,195,138. *Urban:* 52%; *rural:* 48%.
Capital: Raleigh.
Largest cities (1990 census): Charlotte (395,925), Raleigh (212,092), Greensboro (183,894), Winston-Salem (143,532), Durham (136,612), Fayetteville (75,850).
State motto: *Esse Quam Videri* (To be, rather than to seem).
State song: "The Old North State."
State symbols: *Flower*: flowering dogwood; *bird*: cardinal; *tree*: pine.
Land features: Broad plains, which make up two-fifths of the state, border the Atlantic Ocean in the east. Off the coast are low ridges of sand, called bars, that form a barrier against the ocean waves. In the north, the bars enclose a large area of sea called Pamlico Sound. Inland lies the Piedmont Plateau, a hilly area which forms another two-fifths of the state. The west contains ranges of the Appalachian Mountains. This region contains the state's highest point, Mount Mitchell, at 6,684 ft. (2,037 m.). Major rivers include the Roanoke in the north and the Neuse which flows into Pamlico Sound. Forests cover nearly two-thirds of the land.
Climate: Apart from the mountainous west, most of North Carolina has hot summers and mild winters, with abundant precipitation, including rain and melted snow.
Economy: Forests, fertile soils, and building stone are the state's chief natural resources. Farmland covers more than a third of the land. Leading animal products include broilers, hogs, and turkeys. The major crops are tobacco, corn, soybeans, peanuts, and sweet potatoes. Manufacturing is important and manufactures

include tobacco products, textiles, chemicals, electrical and electronic equipment, and machinery, including computers. However, service industries account for more than three-fifths of the state's gross product.
Major attractions: Biltmore Estate, near Asheville; Blue Ridge Parkway, which extends into Virginia; Cape Hatteras and Cape Lookout National Seashores; Cherokee Indian Reservation, Cherokee, near Asheville; Great Smoky Mountains National Park, which extends into Tennessee; Wright Brothers

National Memorial, near Kitty Hawk in the northeast.
Famous North Carolinians: Richard J. Gatling, Billy Graham, Presidents Andrew Johnson and James K. Polk, Thomas Wolfe.

KEY DATES

1524 *The Italian explorer Giovanni da Verrazano, representing France, sailed along the state's coast.*
1585 *An English settlement was founded on Roanoke Island; it later disappeared for unknown reasons.*
1650 *The first permanent settlers arrived from Virginia.*
1765 *Settlers in North Carolina began to oppose British tax laws.*
1789 *North Carolina became the 12th state of the Union.*
1861 *North Carolina seceded from the Union and supported the Confederacy.*
1868 *North Carolina was readmitted to the Union.*
1903 *The Wright brothers made the first successful flight in a power-driven airplane.*

Chimney Rock, looking toward Hickory Nut Gorge.

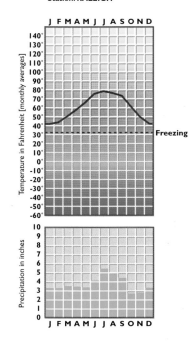

NORTH CAROLINA
Station: RALEIGH

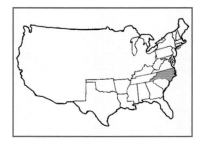

Oklahoma

Oklahoma, one of the Southwestern States, was nicknamed the Sooner State, for settlers who were there "sooner" than the land was opened. Oklahoma ranks 18th in area and 27th in population.

Area: 69,956 sq. miles (181,185 sq. km.).
Population (1995): 3,277,687. *Urban:* 67%; *rural:* 33%.
Capital: Oklahoma City.
Largest cities (1990 census): Oklahoma City (444,724), Tulsa (367,302), Lawton (80,561), Norman (80,071).
State motto: *Labor Omnia Vincit* (Labor conquers all things).
State song: "Oklahoma!"
State symbols: *Flower:* mistletoe; *bird:* scissor-tailed flycatcher; *tree:* redbud.
Land features: Oklahoma has varied scenery. The main upland areas are the Ozark Plateau in the northeast, the Ouachita Mountains in the southeast, and the Arbuckle Mountains and the Wichita Mountains in the south. But the state's highest point, Black Mesa, reaches 4,973 ft. (1,516 m.) in the Great Plains region in the northwest. Between the upland areas are plains and hill country containing grassy prairie and farmland. Major rivers include the Red River, which forms the southern border, and the Arkansas River in the northeast. Forests cover about one-fifth of the land.
Climate: Oklahoma has hot summers and cool winters. The precipitation, including rain and melted snow, varies from about 50 inches (1270 mm.) in the southeast to 15 inches (381 mm.) in the northwest.

Economy: Oklahoma is one of the leading states in producing oil and natural gas. Cattle ranching is important and beef cattle are the state's most valuable agricultural product. Major crops include wheat and hay, while others include cotton, peanuts, pecans, grain sorghum, and soybeans. Manufactures include transport equipment, machinery, electrical and electronic equipment, and processed foods. However, service industries account for about

seven-tenths of the state's gross product.
Major attractions: Cherokee Heritage Center, Tahlequah; Chickasaw National Recreation Area, in south-central Oklahoma; Thomas Gilcrease Institute of American History and Art, Tulsa; Will Rogers Memorial, Claremore, northeast of Tulsa.
Famous Oklahomans: Ralph Ellison, Will Rogers, Maria Tallchief, Jim Thorpe.

KEY DATES

1541 The Spanish explorer Francisco Vásquez de Coronado reached the area, looking for gold.
1682 Oklahoma was claimed for France as part of the huge colony of Louisiana.
1762 France gave Louisiana colony to Spain.
1800 France again took over Louisiana.
1803 The United States bought Oklahoma as part of the Louisiana Purchase.
1830-2 The Five Civilized Tribes (Cherokee, Chickasaw, Choctaw, Creek, and Seminole) were moved to Oklahoma along the "Trail of Tears."
1889 Part of the state was opened to white settlement.
1890 The Territory of Oklahoma was created.
1907 Oklahoma became the 46th state of the Union.
1928 The Oklahoma City oil field began to operate.

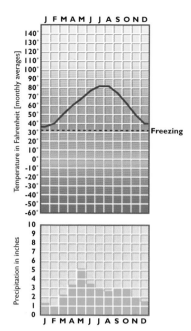
OKLAHOMA
Station: OKLAHOMA CITY

Turner Falls.

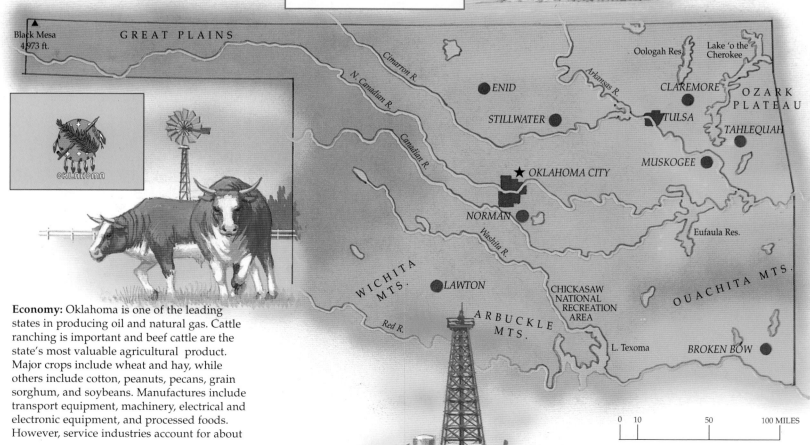

Pennsylvania

Pennsylvania, one of the Middle Atlantic States, is nicknamed the Keystone State, because it was the "keystone" of the original 13 American states. Today, it is the 33rd largest, but ranks 5th in population.

Area: 46,043 sq. km. (119,251 sq. km.).
Population (1995): 12,071,842. *Urban:* 69%; *rural:* 31%.
Capital: Harrisburg.
Largest cities (1990 census): Philadelphia (1,585,577), Pittsburgh (369,879), Erie (108,718), Allentown (105,718), Scranton (81,805), Reading (78,380).
State motto: Virtue, Liberty, and Independence.
State song: None.
State symbols: *Flower:* mountain laurel; *bird:* ruffed grouse; *tree:* hemlock.
Land features: Apart from the Piedmont Plateau, a region of plains and hills in the southeast, most of the state forms part of the Appalachian Mountain system. It includes part of the Blue Mountains in the south and the large Appalachian, or Allegheny, Plateau. The state's highest point is Mount Davis, which reaches 3,213 ft. (979 m.) in the southwest. In the northwest, the Appalachian Plateau descends to the shores of Lake Erie. The main rivers are the Ohio and its tributaries in the west, and the Susqehanna in the center and west. Forests cover about 60% of the land.
Climate: Pennsylvania has cold winters and warm summers. The precipitation, including rain and melted snow, is abundant and occurs throughout the year.
Economy: The chief natural resources include coal and fertile soils and the state is one the leading coal-producing states. The chief manufactures are processed foods, chemicals, and machinery, including computers. Farmland covers about a third of the state. Dairy farming is a major activity, and milk is a leading product. Farmers also raise beef cattle, poultry, and hogs. The chief crops are corn and hay. Greenhouse and nursery products are important, as also are fruits and vegetables. However, service industries account for about three-quarters of the state's gross product.
Major attractions: Allegheny National Forest; Gettysburg National Military Park, near the border with Maryland; Independence National Historical Park, Philadelphia; Valley Forge National Historical Park, near Philadelphia.
Famous Pennsylvanians: Marian Anderson, Maxwell Anderson, President James Buchanan, Stephen Foster, Robert E. Peary, Betsy Ross.

KEY DATES

1643   *Swedes founded the first permanent white settlement in Pennsylvania, near present-day Philadelphia.*
1655   *The Dutch took control of the area.*
1664   *The English took over from the Dutch.*
1681   *The English Charles II granted Pennsylvania to the Quaker William Penn.*
1776   *Congress adopted the Declaration of Independence in what is now Independence Hall, Philadelphia.*
1787   *Pennsylvania became the 2nd state of the Union.*
1863   *Union armies defeated Confederate forces in the Battle of Gettysburg.*
1979   *Scientists prevented a major disaster when an accident occurred at the Three Mile Island nuclear reactor, in Middletown.*

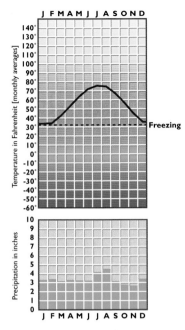

PENNSYLVANIA
Station: PHILADELPHIA

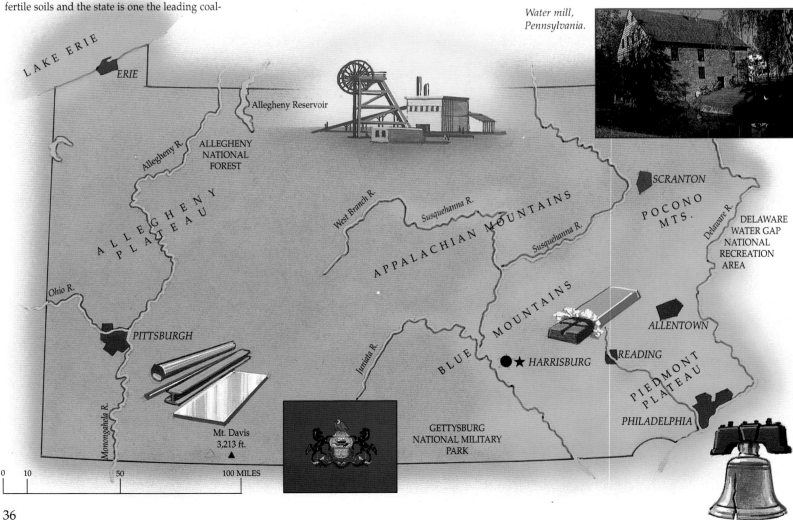

Water mill, Pennsylvania.

Rhode Island

Rhode Island, in New England, whose nicknames are the Ocean State (official) or Little Rhody (unofficial), is the smallest state in the United States. It ranks 43rd in population.

Area: 1,212 sq. miles (3,139 sq. km.).
Population (1995): 989,794. *Urban:* 87%; *rural:* 13%.
Capital: Providence.
Largest cities (1990 census): Providence (160,728), Warwick (85,427), Cranston (76,060), Pawtucket (72,644).
State motto: Hope.
State song: "Rhode Island."
State symbols: *Flower:* violet; *bird:* Rhode Island Red; *tree:* red maple.
Land features: Behind the coast on the Atlantic Ocean lies a broad plain which makes up more than half the state's area. The land rises to the northwest, which contains the state's highest point, Jerimoth Hill, at 812 ft. (247 m.). Rhode Island contains 36 islands, the largest of which is also called Rhode Island. The state has many lakes and ponds, including Scituate Reservoir, the largest inland body of water, together with short, but mostly fast-flowing rivers, several of which have waterfalls. Forests cover about 60% of the land.
Climate: The state has warm summers and mild winters, though average temperatures fall to around or just below freezing point in three winter months. The precipitation, including rain and melted snow, is abundant. Hurricanes sometimes cause great damage.
Economy: The state has few natural resources. Manufacturing is a leading activity and manufactures include costume jewelry, metal products, and scientific instruments. Greenhouse and nursery products, such as ornamental shrubs, are important and milk is the leading farm product. The chief crops are potatoes and hay, while apples are the chief fruit. Fishing and poultry raising are important activities, and the state is known for a type of chicken called the Rhode Island Red. However, service industries account for about three-quarters of the state's gross product.

Major attractions: Coastal resorts, such as Block Island, Narragansett, Newport, and Watch Hill; colonial architecture in many towns; Newport mansions.
Famous Rhode Islanders: George M. Cohan, Nathanael Greene, Matthew C. Perry, Oliver H. Perry, Gilbert Stuart.

KEY DATES

1524 The Italian explorer Giovanni da Verrazano, representing France, reached Narragansett Bay.
1636 The first white settlement was founded at Providence.
1776 Rhode Island declared its independence from England.
1790 Rhode Island became the 13th state of theUnion.
1861-5 About 24,000 Rhode Islanders served in the Union forces during the Civil War.
1938 A powerful hurricane caused great loss of life.

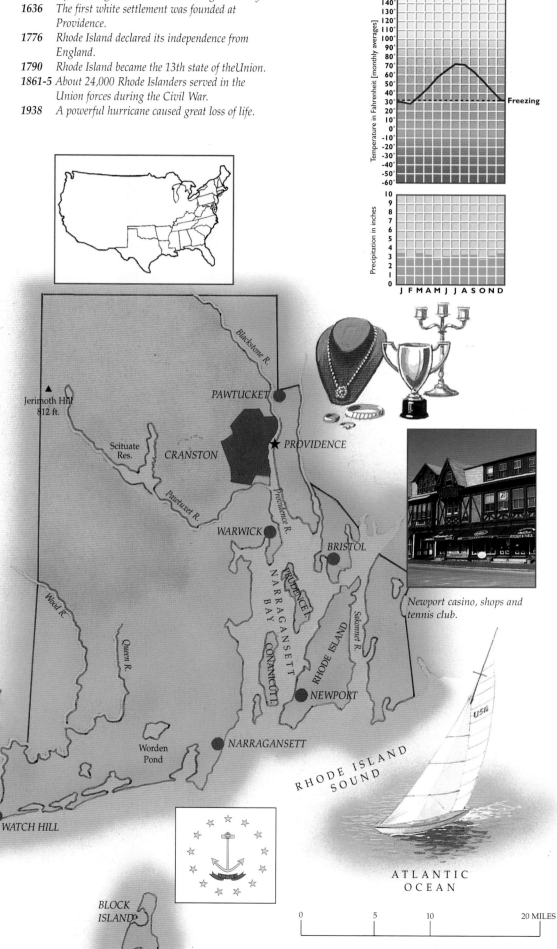

Newport casino, shops and tennis club.

South Carolina

South Carolina, one of the Southern States, is nicknamed the Palmetto State. It is the 40th largest, but ranks 26th in population.

Area: 31,113 sq. miles (80,582 sq. km.).
Population (1995): 3,673,287. *Urban:* 54%; *rural:* 46%.
Capital: Columbia.
Largest cities (1990 census): Columbia (103,477), Charleston (79,925), North Charleston (close to Charleston and not shown on the map, 70,304), Greenville (58,256).
State mottoes: *Animis Opibusque Parati* (Prepared in mind and resources); *Dum Spiro Spero* (While I breathe, I hope).
State song: "Carolina."
State symbols: *Flower*: Carolina jessamine; *bird*: Carolina wren; *tree*: palmetto.
Land features: The plains that border the Atlantic Ocean make up the state's largest region. Inland lies the Piedmont Plateau, which slopes upwards to the Blue Ridge Mountains in the far northwest. These mountains contain the state's highest peak, Sassafras Mountain, which reaches 3,560 ft. (1,085 m.).

The main rivers include the Savannah, which forms the border with Georgia, the Santee in central South Carolina, and the Pee Dee in the northeast. Forests cover about two-thirds of the land.
Climate: South Carolina has hot summers and mild winters. The precipitation, which mainly takes the form of rain, is abundant. The state lies in the path of hurricanes which form in the Atlantic Ocean.
Economy: Natural resources include fertile soils, forests, plentiful water, and building stone. The main crops are tobacco and soybeans, while corn, cotton, hay, and wheat are also grown. Fruits (especially peaches), and vegetables are also important. Beef cattle, milk, and poultry are other leading products, while fishing, notably for shrimp, is an important activity. Manufactures include textiles, chemicals, paper products, and

machinery. However, service industries account for nearly seven-tenths of the state's gross product.
Major attractions: Cowpens National Battlefield in the northwest; Cypress Gardens and other gardens around Charleston; Fort Sumter National Monument in Charleston Harbor; Kings Mountain National Military Park in the northwest; seaside resorts, such as Myrtle Beach.
Famous South Carolinians: President Andrew Jackson (though he may been born in North Carolina), Jesse Jackson, Francis Marion, John B. Watson.

KEY DATES

1521 Spanish explorers reached the coast of what is now South Carolina.
1670 Englishmen founded the first permanent white settlement in South Carolina.
1780 American forces were victorious in the Battle of Kings Mountain, a major victory in the Revolutionary War.
1788 South Carolina became the 8th state of the Union.
1860 The state seceded from the Union.
1861 The Civil War began when Confederate forces fired on Fort Sumter in Charleston Harbor.
1868 South Carolina was readmitted to the Union.
1941 Santee Dam was completed.
1989 Hurricane Hugo caused great damage in South Carolina; 18 people were killed.

SOUTH CAROLINA
Station: CHARLESTON

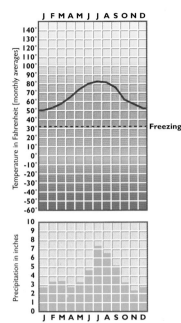

East Battery house, Charleston.

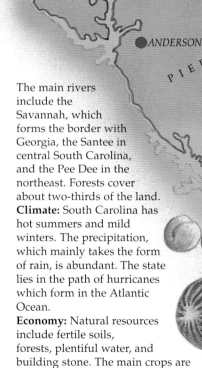

Tennessee

Tennessee, one of the Southern States, is nicknamed the Volunteer State. It is the 34th largest state, but it ranks 17th in population.

Area: 42,144 sq. miles (109,152 sq. km.).
Population (1995): 5,256,051. *Urban:* 60%; *rural:* 40%.
Capital: Nashville.
Largest cities (1990 census): Memphis (610,337), Nashville (488,374), Knoxville (165,039), Chattanooga (152,393), Clarksville (75,542).
State motto: Agriculture and Commerce.
State song: "The Tennessee Waltz."
State symbols: *Flower:* iris; *bird:* mockingbird; *tree:* tulip poplar.
Land features: The Appalachian Mountain system, in eastern Tennessee, includes part of the Blue Ridge Mountains, the Appalachian range and valley region, and the Cumberland Plateau. The state's highest point, Clingmans Dome, reaches 6,643 ft. (2,025 m.) in the Blue Ridge Mountains. West of the Cumberland Plateau lies a high plain, which surrounds the Nashville basin. In the west, flood plains border the Mississippi River, which forms the state's western border. Other major waterways include the Cumberland and Tennessee rivers. Many dams, with hydroelectric plants, have been built by the T.V.A. (Tennessee Valley Authority). They hold back many reservoirs. Forests cover about half of the land.
Climate: Apart from the higher areas, most of the state has a subtropical climate, with hot summers and mild winters. The state has abundant precipitation, including rain and, especially in the east, melted snow.
Economy: The state's natural resources include fertile soils, abundant water supplies, and coal. Farmland covers about half of the state. Many farmers raise beef and dairy cattle, while hogs, poultry, and horses are also important. The chief crops are corn, cotton, hay, soybeans, and tobacco. Major manufactures are chemicals and chemical products, processed food products, transport equipment, and industrial machinery and equipment. Service industries account for about seven-tenths of the state's gross product.
Major attractions: Andrew Johnson National Historic Site, Greeneville; Big South Fork National River and Recreation area, which extends into Kentucky; Chickamauga and Chattanooga National Military Park, which extends into Georgia; Fort Donelson National Battlefield, west of Clarksville; Graceland, Elvis Presley's estate, Memphis; Great Smoky Mountains National Park, which extends into North Carolina; Opryland, U.S.A., near Nashville; Stones River National Battlefield, Murfreesboro.
Famous Tennesseans: Davy Crockett, Cordell Hull, Bessie Smith, Alvin York.

KEY DATES

1540	*The Spanish explorer Hernando de Soto reached what is now Tennessee.*
1682	*The Mississippi valley was claimed for France.*
1763	*France passed over to Britain its claims on lands east of the Mississippi River.*
1796	*Tennessee became the 16th state of the Union.*
1861	*Tennessee seceded from the Union.*
1866	*Tennessee was readmitted to the Union.*
1933	*The Tennessee Valley Authority was created.*
1942	*Work began at Oak Ridge on the world's first nuclear reactor.*

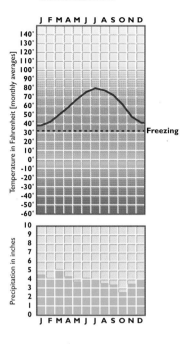

TENNESSEE
Station: NASHVILLE

Reelfoot Lake, Tennessee.

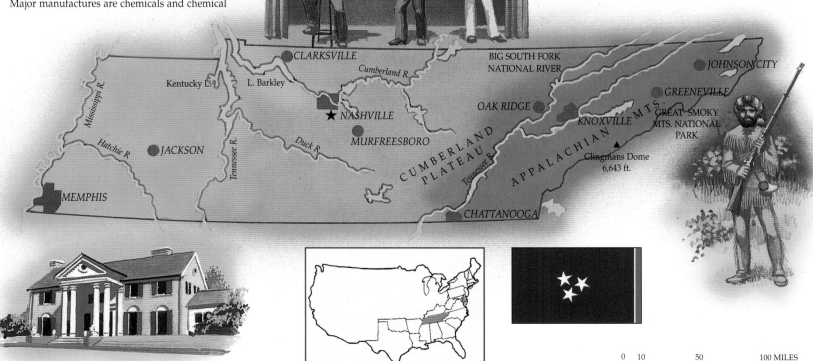

Elvis Presley's house, Graceland.

Texas

The Southwestern State of Texas, the Lone Star State, ranks second only to Alaska in size and only California has a larger population.

Area: 266,807 sq. miles (691,027 sq. km.).
Population (1995): 18,723,991. *Urban*: 80%; *rural*: 20%.
Capital: Austin.
Largest cities (1990 census): Houston (1,629,902); Dallas (1,007,608); San Antonio (935,393); El Paso (515,342); Austin (465,648); Fort Worth (447,619).
State motto: Friendship.
State song: "Texas, Our Texas."
State symbols: *Flower*: bluebonnet; *bird*: mockingbird; *tree*: pecan.
Land features: The Gulf Coastal Plains in the south and southeast rise inland to flat prairies and hill country. Part of the Great Plains lies in the west and northwest, while the Basin and Range region, also called the Trans-Pecos region, lies in the southwest. This contains the state's highest point, Guadalupe Peak, at 8,751 ft. (2,667 m.). The longest river, the Rio Grande, flows along the Mexican border. Forests cover 16% of the state.
Climate: The climate ranges from subtropical in the southeast to temperate in the northwest. The average annual rainfall decreases from around 47 inches (1200 mm.) in the northeast to 12 inches (300 mm.) in the west.
Economy: Oil and natural gas form the basis of the state's economy, but Texas also has large aircraft, oil refining, and food processing industries. Beef cattle are the leading livestock while major crops include cotton, grain sorghum, hay, wheat, citrus and other fruits, peanuts, pecans, and vegetables. Service industries account for about two-thirds of the state's gross product.
Major attractions: Big Bend and Guadalupe Mountains national parks; Padre Island National Seashore; Fort Davis, Palo Alto Battlefield, and Lyndon B. Johnson national historic sites; the Alamo and Mission San Jose (San Antonio); and the Lyndon B. Johnson Space Center (Houston). Other attractions include two amusement parks – Astroworld (Houston) and Six Flags over Texas (at Arlington, west of Dallas) – and the Texas Ranger Hall of Fame (Waco).
Famous Texans: Lloyd M. Bentsen Jr., Dwight D. Eisenhower, Howard Hughes, Lyndon B. Johnson, Chester Nimitz, Katherine Anne Porter.

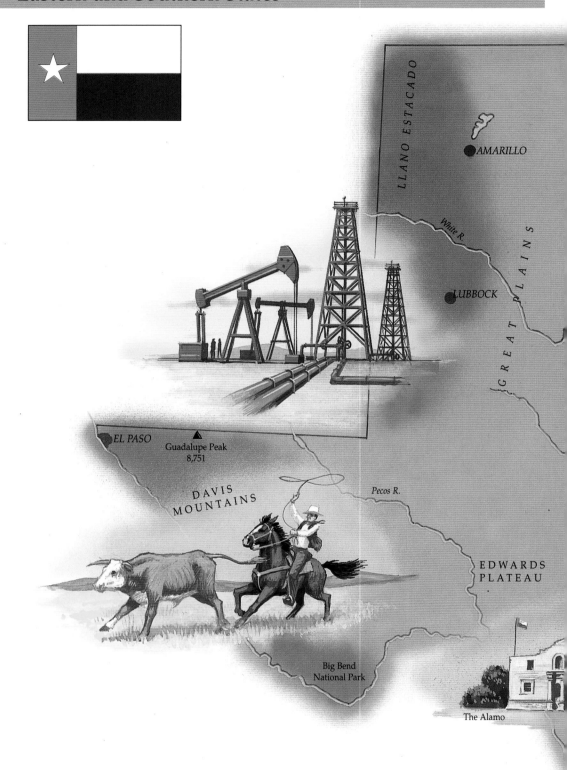

KEY DATES

1519 *The Spanish mapped the coast of Texas.*
1682 *Spanish missionaries found the first European settlements near present-day San Antonio.*
1821 *Mexico became independent and Texas became part of the Mexican empire; Americans settled in Texas.*
1835 *The Mexican army defeated an American force at the Alamo, but the Americans defeated the Mexicans at the Battle of Jacinto. Texas became an independent republic.*
1845 *Texas became the 28th state of the United States.*
1861 *Texas seceded and joined the Confederacy.*
1870 *Texas rejoined the Union.*
1901 *Oil was discovered near Beaumont.*
1963 *Lyndon B. Johnson became the 36th president of the U.S., following the murder of President John F. Kennedy in Dallas on November 22.*
1960s *Texas began to play a leading role in the U.S. space program.*

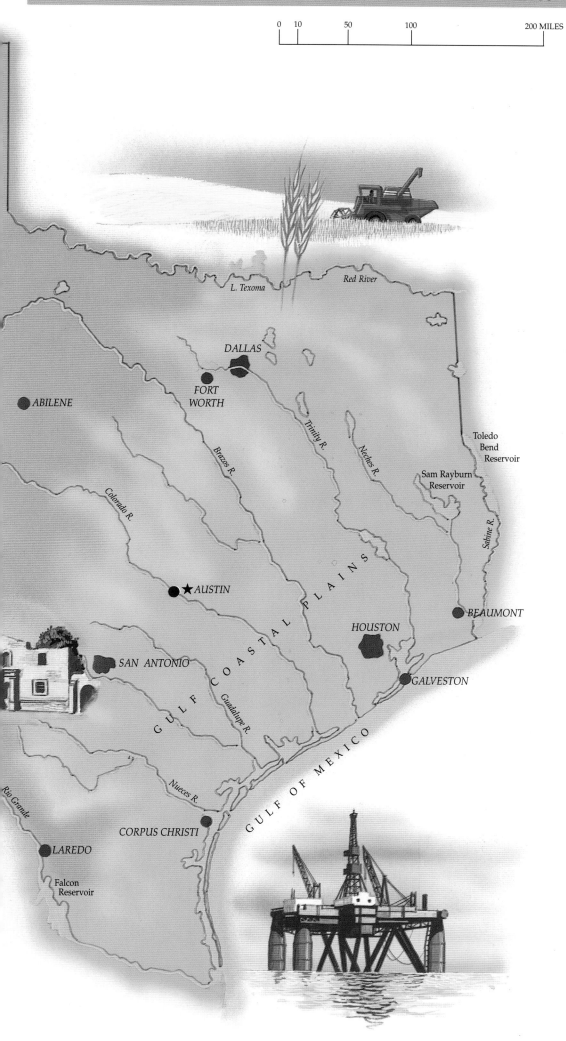

0 10   50   100   200 MILES

L. Texoma
Red River
DALLAS
FORT WORTH
ABILENE
Brazos R.
Trinity R.
Neches R.
Toledo Bend Reservoir
Sam Rayburn Reservoir
Sabine R.
Colorado R.
AUSTIN
G U L F   C O A S T A L   P L A I N S
BEAUMONT
HOUSTON
SAN ANTONIO
Guadalupe R.
GALVESTON
G U L F   O F   M E X I C O
Rio Grande
Nueces R.
CORPUS CHRISTI
LAREDO
Falcon Reservoir

Space Center rocket, Houston.

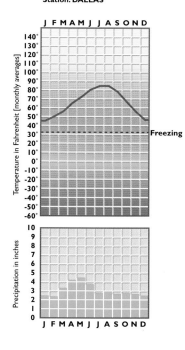

TEXAS
Station: DALLAS

J F M A M J J A S O N D

140°
130°
120°
110°
100°
90°
80°
70°
60°
50°
40°
30°
20°
10°
0°
-10°
-20°
-30°
-40°
-50°
-60°

Temperature in Fahrenheit [monthly averages]

Freezing

10
9
8
7
6
5
4
3
2
1
0

Precipitation in inches

J F M A M J J A S O N D

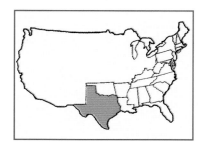

Vermont

Vermont, in New England, is nicknamed the Green Mountain State (Vermont means "green mountain" in French). It ranks 43rd in area and 49th in population.

Area: 9,614 sq. miles (24,900 sq. km.).
Population (1995): 584,771. *Urban:* 66%; *rural:* 34%.
Capital: Montpelier.
Largest cities: Burlington (39,127), Rutland (18,230).
State motto: Freedom and Unity.
State song: "Hail, Vermont."
State symbols: *Flower:* red clover; *bird:* hermit thrush; *tree:* sugar maple.
Land features: Apart from a lowland area bordering Lake Champlain in the northwest, most of Vermont consists of scenic uplands. The Green Mountains, which run north-south through the state, contain Vermont's highest point, Mount Mansfield, which reaches 4,393 ft. (1,339 m.). The Connecticut River forms the state's eastern border and it is fed by many small rivers that rise in the Green Mountains. Lake Champlain, which extends into New York and Quebec, is the largest lake, but there are several hundred smaller lakes and ponds. Forests cover about three-quarters of the land.
Climate: Vermont has short but warm summers and long, cold, snowy winters. The snow is important and the state has numerous ski resorts, which attract many tourists in winter.
Economy: Vermont's natural resources include some fertile land (mainly in the valleys), forests, and building stone. Farmland covers about 25% of the state and dairy farming is the leading activity. Beef cattle are also raised and the state is known for its maple syrup. Crops include corn, fruits (especially apples), hay, and vegetables, including potatoes. Manufacturing is important, especially electrical and electronic equipment – IBM has a large plant in the Burlington area. Other manufactures include metal products (including guns), printed materials, machinery (including computers), and processed food products. However, service industries account for about seven-tenths of the state's gross product.
Major attractions: Coolidge Birthplace, Plymouth, southeast of Rutland; Green Mountain National Forest; ski resorts; Stowe winter carnival in January.
Famous Vermonters: Presidents Chester A. Arthur and Calvin Coolidge, John Dewey, Stephen A. Douglas, John Fisk.

KEY DATES

1609 The area that is now Vermont was claimed for France by the French explorer Samuel de Champlain.
1763 Britain gained control of Vermont following the French and Indian War (1754-63).
1775 Ethan Allen and a group of settlers called the Green Mountain Boys, captured Fort Ticonderoga on the western shore of Lake Champlain in the Revolutionary War.
1777 Vermont was declared a republic.
1791 Vermont became the 14th state of the Union.
1881 The Vermonter Chester A. Arthur became the 21st president of the United States.
1923 The Vermonter Calvin Coolidge became the 30th president of the United States.

Woodstock.

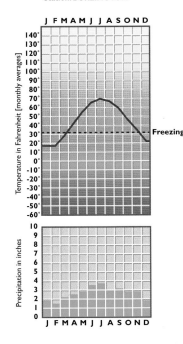

VERMONT
Station: BURLINGTON

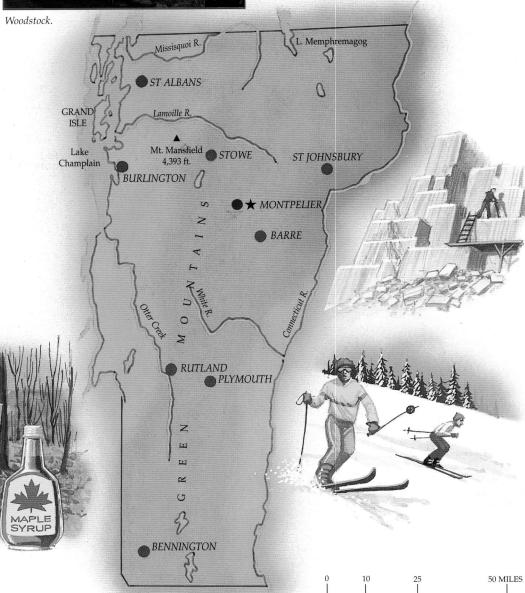

| 0 | 10 | 25 | 50 MILES |

Virginia

Virginia, one of the Southern States, is nicknamed the Old Dominion, a name given to it by King Charles II because it stayed loyal to the crown in the English Civil War. Virginia is the 36th largest state, but ranks 12th in population.

Area: 40,767 sq. miles (105,586 sq. km.).
Population (1995): 6,618,358. *Urban:* 66%; *rural:* 34%.
Capital: Richmond.
Largest cities: Virginia Beach (393,089), Norfolk (261,250), Richmond (202,798), Newport News (171,439), Arlington (170,936).
State motto: *Sic Semper Tyrannis* (Thus always to tyrants).
State song: "Carry Me Back To Old Virginia."
State symbols: *Flower:* flowering dogwood; *bird:* cardinal; *tree:* flowering dogwood.
Land features: Eastern Virginia is a lowlying region facing the Atlantic Ocean. Inland lies the Piedmont Plateau, which slopes up towards the Appalachian Mountain system. The state's highest peak, Mount Rogers, reaches 5,729 ft. (1,746 m.) in the Blue Ridge Mountains, a range of the Appalachians. Major rivers include the Potomac, which forms the state's northeastern boundary, and the James, which flows through Richmond. Forests cover more than three-fifths of the land.
Climate: Virginia has warm to hot summers and wild winters. The precipitation, including rain and melted snow, ranges from about 35 to 45 inches (889-1143 mm.).
Economy: Natural resources include some fertile soils, coal, and building stone. Beef cattle are important products, and farmers also produce milk, chickens, and turkeys. Major crops include apples, corn, hay, peanuts, soybeans, and, especially, tobacco. Manufactures include chemicals, tobacco products, transportation equipment, and processed food products. Service industries account for around three-quarters of the state's gross product.

Major attractions: Appomattox Court House National Historical Park; Booker T. Washington National Monument, near Roanoke; Colonial National Historical Park, including Jamestown and nearby Williamsburg and Yorktown; Cumberland Gap National Historical Park; George Washington Birthplace National Monument; Jamestown Festival Park; Mount Vernon; Shenandoah National Park in the Blue Ridge Mountains.
Famous Virginians: Presidents George Washington, Thomas Jefferson, James Madison, William H. Harrison, John Tyler, Zachary Taylor, and Woodrow Wilson. Other famous Virginians include Richard E. Byrd, the explorers William Clark and Meriwether Lewis, Patrick Henry, Robert E. Lee, and Booker T. Washington.

KEY DATES

1607 *The colony of Jamestown was established.*
1624 *Virginia became an English colony.*
1776 *Virginia declared its independence.*
1781 *The British surrendered at Yorktown, ending the Revolutionary War.*
1788 *Virginia became the 10th state of the Union.*
1789 *The Virginian George Washington became the first president of the United States.*
1861 *Virginia seceded from the Union and joined the Confederacy.*
1870 *Virginia was readmitted to the Union.*
1912 *Woodrow Wilson became the eighth Virginian to be elected President of the United States.*

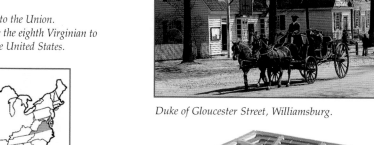

VIRGINIA
Station: NORFOLK

Duke of Gloucester Street, Williamsburg.

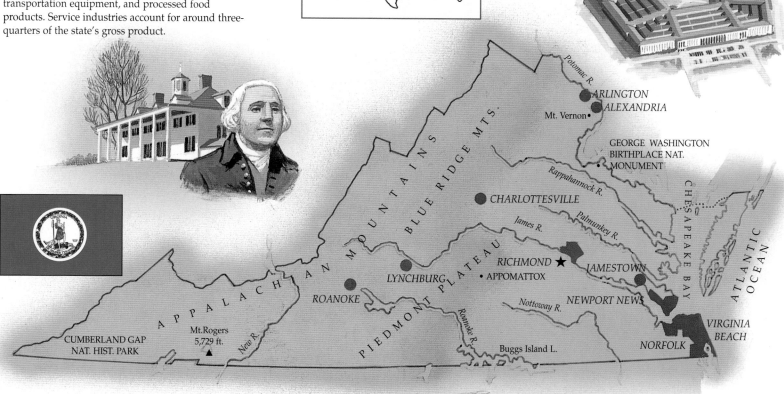

King Street, Alexandria, Virginia.

West Virginia

West Virginia, one of the Southern States, is nicknamed the Mountain State because of its rugged scenery. It is the 41st largest state, and ranks 35th in population.

Area: 24,232 sq, miles (62,760 sq. km.).
Population (1995): 1,828,140. *Urban:* 64%; *rural:* 36%.
Capital: Charleston.
Largest cities: Charleston (57,287), Huntington (54,844), Wheeling (34,882), Parkersburg (33,862).
State motto: *Montani Semper Liberi* (Mountaineers are always free).
State song: "The West Virginia Hills."
State symbols: *Flower:* rhododendron; *bird:* cardinal; *tree:* sugar maple.
Land features: West Virginia is a landlocked state which lies within the Appalachian Mountain system. The highest point, Spruce Knob, reaches 4,863 ft. (1,482 m.) in the Allegheny Mountains in the southeast. West of this region lies the Allegheny Plateau, the largest land region. Most of the rivers are tributaries of the Ohio River, which forms much of the state's western border. Forests cover about four-fifths of the area.
Climate: West Virginia has warm summers and cold winters, especially in the higher areas. The precipitation, including rain and melted snow, is abundant.
Economy: The state's natural resources include coal and fertile soils, especially in river valleys. Coal mining is an important source of income, and some natural gas, oil, and building stone are also to be found. The production of chemicals, using local coal and other minerals, is the leading manufacturing industry. The state also produces metals, including steel, and stone, clay, and glass products. Farmland covers about a quarter of the state. Beef cattle and milk are the leading farm products and hay is the chief crop. The state also produces corn, tobacco, and wheat, together with such fruits as apples and peaches. However, service industries account for nearly seven-tenths of the state's gross product.
Major attractions: Chesapeake and Ohio Canal, and Harpers Ferry national historical parks, both of which are on the border with Maryland; southern West Virginia contains the Bluestone National Scenic River, the Gauley River National Recreation Area, and the New River Gorge National River.
Famous West Virginians: Pearl Buck, Thomas "Stonewall" Jackson, Cyrus Vance, Charles E. Yeager.

KEY DATES

1624 *Virginia, including what is now West Virginia, became an English colony.*
1727 *Germans from Pennsylvania founded a settlement in West Virginia.*
1742 *Coal was discovered in West Virginia.*
1859 *John Brown and his followers, hoping to start a slave rebellion, seized the federal arsenal at Harpers Ferry.*
1861 *The counties of West Virginia refused to secede from the Union with Virginia.*
1863 *West Virginia became the 35th state of the Union.*
1959 *The National Radio Astronomy, or Green Bank, Observatory started operations in West Virginia.*

A Farm near Morgantown near West Virginia.

WEST VIRGINIA
Station: CHARLESTON

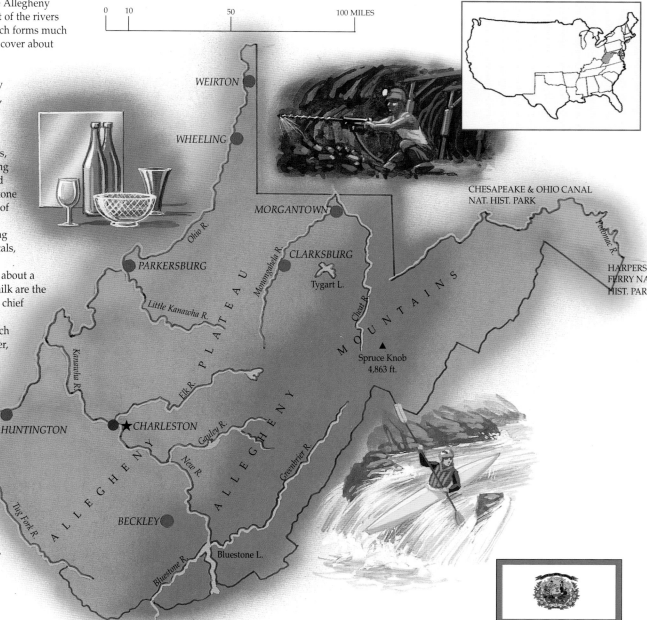

Midwestern States

Rodeo, Iowa.

The 12 Midwestern States sprawl across a vast area of rolling plains that stretch from the Appalachian Mountains to the Rockies. The region contains parts of four of the five Great Lakes and the valleys of the Mississippi and Missouri rivers.

During the last Ice Age, which ended only about 10,000 years ago, ice sheets spread over much of the land. These ice sheets were important in shaping the landscape, especially by carving out the Great Lakes and many other small basins in Michigan, Minnesota, and Wisconsin that now contain sparkling lakes. To the south, in parts of Illinois, Iowa, Indiana, and Ohio, the ice sheets deposited boulder clay. These areas are now fertile farmland where rich harvests of corn and wheat are gathered.

To the west, the land rises gradually to the Great or High Plains, a dry prairie region grazed by cattle and other livestock and where isolated uplands break up their monotony. The uplands include the Black Hills of South Dakota, where the carved heads of George Washington, Thomas Jefferson, Theodore Roosevelt, and Abraham Lincoln look down benignly from a granite cliff at the Mount Rushmore National Memorial. Southwestern South Dakota also contains such historic sites as Deadwood, an Old West mining town, and Wounded Knee, site of the last major battle between the Native Americans and white men.

The Midwest is a major farming region, but it also contains several great cities. Chicago, Illinois, the nation's third largest city behind New York City and Los Angeles, is a major manufacturing and cultural center. Other Midwestern cities that number among the 25 largest in the United States are Detroit, Michigan, which is often called "The Automobile Capital of the World," Indianapolis, Indiana, which is famed for its Indianapolis 500 automobile race, together with two leading manufacturing cities: Columbus, Ohio; and Milwaukee, Wisconsin.

Buffalo ranch, South Dakota.

N. DAKOTA

MINNESOTA

L. Superior

MICHIGAN

L. Huron

S. DAKOTA

WISCONSIN

L. Michigan

L. Ontario

Mississippi R.

Missouri R.

IOWA

L. Erie

NEBRASKA

INDIANA

OHIO

ILLINOIS

KANSAS

MISSOURI

Mark Twain's house, Hannibal, Missouri.

Illinois

Illinois, one of the Midwestern States, is nicknamed the Land of Lincoln or the Prairie State. It ranks 24th in area, but comes 6th in population.

Area: 57,871 sq. miles (149,885 sq. km.).
Population (1995): 11,829,940. *Urban:* 83%; *rural:* 17%.
Capital: Springfield.
Largest cities (1990 census): Chicago (2,783,726), Rockford (139,704), Peoria (113,504), Springfield (105,417).
State motto: State Sovereignty, National Union.
State song: "Illinois."
State symbols: *Flower*: native violet; *bird*: cardinal; *tree*: white oak.
Land features: Illinois forms part of a large land region called the Interior Plains. Much of the land is covered by moraine, i.e., soil and rock dumped there by ice sheets during the Ice Age, which ended only 10,000 years ago. A small area in the northwest, which was not covered by the ice, contains the state's highest point, Charles Mound, at 1,235 ft. (376 m.). The Mississippi River forms the state's western border. A canal links Lake Michigan to the Mississippi River, via the Illinois River, one of the tributaries of the Mississippi. Forests cover only about a tenth of the land.
Climate: Located far from the sea, Illinois has a severe climate with cold, snowy winters and hot summers. Tornadoes sometimes cause great damage.
Economy: The state's natural resources are its fertile soils, coal, and oil. Illinois is one of the leading manufacturing states. Machinery includes construction and farm equipment, and machine tools. Also important are processed foods, chemical products, printed materials, metal products, and electrical and electronic equipment. Farmland covers about 75% of the state. The chief crops are corn, soybeans, hay, and wheat. Hogs are the leading farm animals. Service industries, which are concentrated mainly in urban areas, especially in and around Chicago, account for about three-quarters of the state's gross product.
Major attractions: Abraham Lincoln's home, Springfield; Cahokia Mounds, the largest Native American mound in the U.S.; Chicago's museums; Illinois State Museum, Springfield; Mormon settlement, Nauvoo, on the Mississippi, west of Peoria; Shawnee National Forest; Ulysses S. Grant home, Galena, in northwestern Illinois.
Famous Illinoisans: Jane Addams, John Dos Passos, Benny Goodman, Ernest Hemingway, Wild Bill Hickok, President Ronald Reagan.

KEY DATES

1699 The French founded Cahokia, the oldest European settlement in Illinois.
1717 Illinois became part of Louisiana, a French colony.
1763 Illinois came under British rule following the French and Indian War.
1783 Illinois became part of the United States.
1818 Illinois became the 21st state of the Union.
1871 Fire destroyed much of Chicago.
1960 One of the nation's biggest nuclear reactors was completed at Morris, near Chicago.

Skyscraper, Chicago.

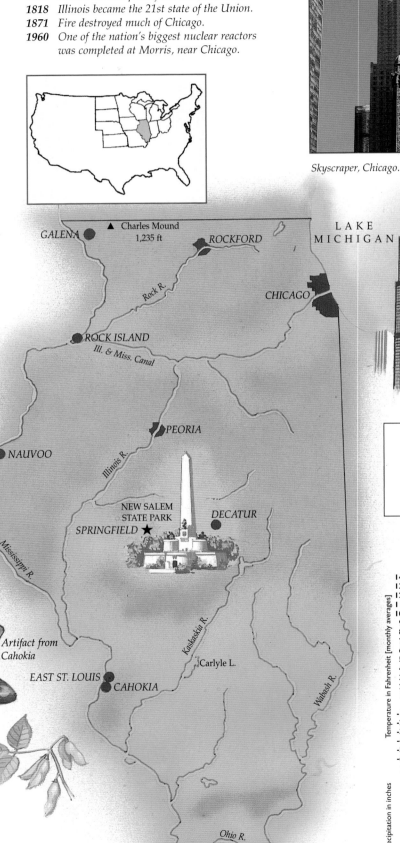

Artifact from Cahokia

ILLINOIS

**ILLINOIS
Station: CHICAGO**

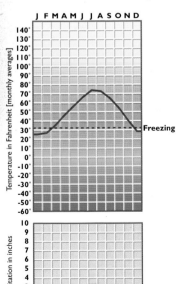

0 10   50   100 MILES

Indiana

Indiana is nicknamed the Hoosier State, possibly for a man called Samuel Hoosier, or it may be a slang expression. Indiana, a Midwestern State, ranks only 38th in area, but comes 14th in population.

Area: 36,413 sq. miles (94,309 sq. km.).
Population (1995): 5,803,471. *Urban*: 64%; *rural*: 36%.
Capital: Indianapolis.
Largest cities (1990 census): Indianapolis (731,327), Fort Wayne (172,971), Evansville (126,272), Gary (116,646), South Bend (105,511).
State motto: The Crossroads of America.
State song: "On the Banks of the Wabash, Far Away."
State symbols: *Flower*: peony; *bird*: cardinal; *tree*: tulip poplar.
Land features: Indiana occupies part of the American Interior Plains and the land is mostly lowlying, reaching a highest point of 1,257 ft. (383 m.) in central Indiana, near the Ohio border. The northern part of the state is largely covered by moraine, soil and rocks dumped there by ice sheets during the Ice Age which ended only 10,000 years ago. Only the hills and plains in the south were not blanketed by ice. The Wabash River and its tributaries drain most of the state, while the Ohio River forms the southern boundary with Kentucky. Forests cover about a sixth of the state.
Climate: Winters are cold and snowy, but the state has warm summers. Droughts and floods sometimes occur, especially in the south.
Economy: Natural resources include fertile soil, plentiful water, and minerals, such as coal and oil, which is produced west of Evansville. The state produces metals, such as steel and aluminum, while other major manufactures include transportation equipment, electrical equipment, and chemical products. Farmland covers about 70% of the state and corn and soybeans are the leading products. Hay, rapeseed, and wheat are important, as also are vegetables. Hogs are the leading farm animals. Service industries, notably the wholesale and retail trade, account for more than three-fifths of the state's gross product,
Major attractions: Historic Fort Wayne; Hoosier National Forest, south of Indianapolis; Indiana Dunes National Lakeshore on Lake Michigan; the Indianapolis 500 automobile race; Lincoln Boyhood National Memorial.
Famous Hoosiers: Hoagy Carmichael, James Dean, Theodore Dreiser, Virgil Grissom, Cole Porter, Kurt Vonnegut Jr., Lew Wallace.

KEY DATES

1679 *Frenchman Robert Cavelier, Sieur de La Salle, became the first European to reach the area.*
1731-2 *The French set up the first permanent settlement at Vincennes.*
1763 *Indiana came under British rule after the French and Indian War.*
1800 *Congress created the Indiana Territory.*
1816 *Indiana became the 19th state of the Union.*
1911 *The first Indianapolis 500 automobile race took place.*
1970 *The Port of Indiana was opened at Burns Harbor on Lake Michigan.*

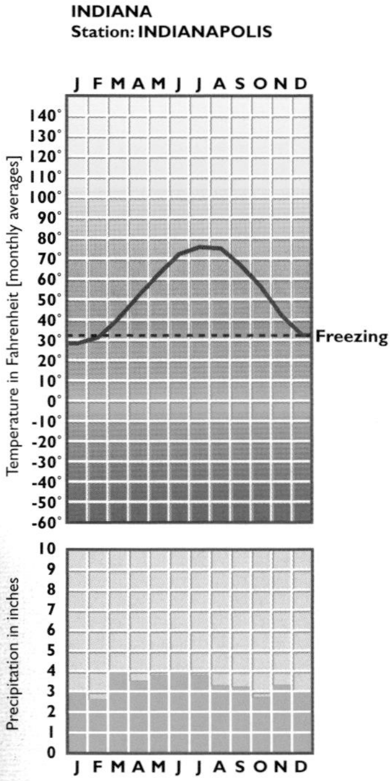
INDIANA
Station: INDIANAPOLIS
J F M A M J J A S O N D
Temperature in Fahrenheit [monthly averages]
140° 130° 120° 110° 100° 90° 80° 70° 60° 50° 40° 30° 20° 10° 0° -10° -20° -30° -40° -50° -60°
Freezing
Precipitation in inches
10 9 8 7 6 5 4 3 2 1 0
J F M A M J J A S O N D

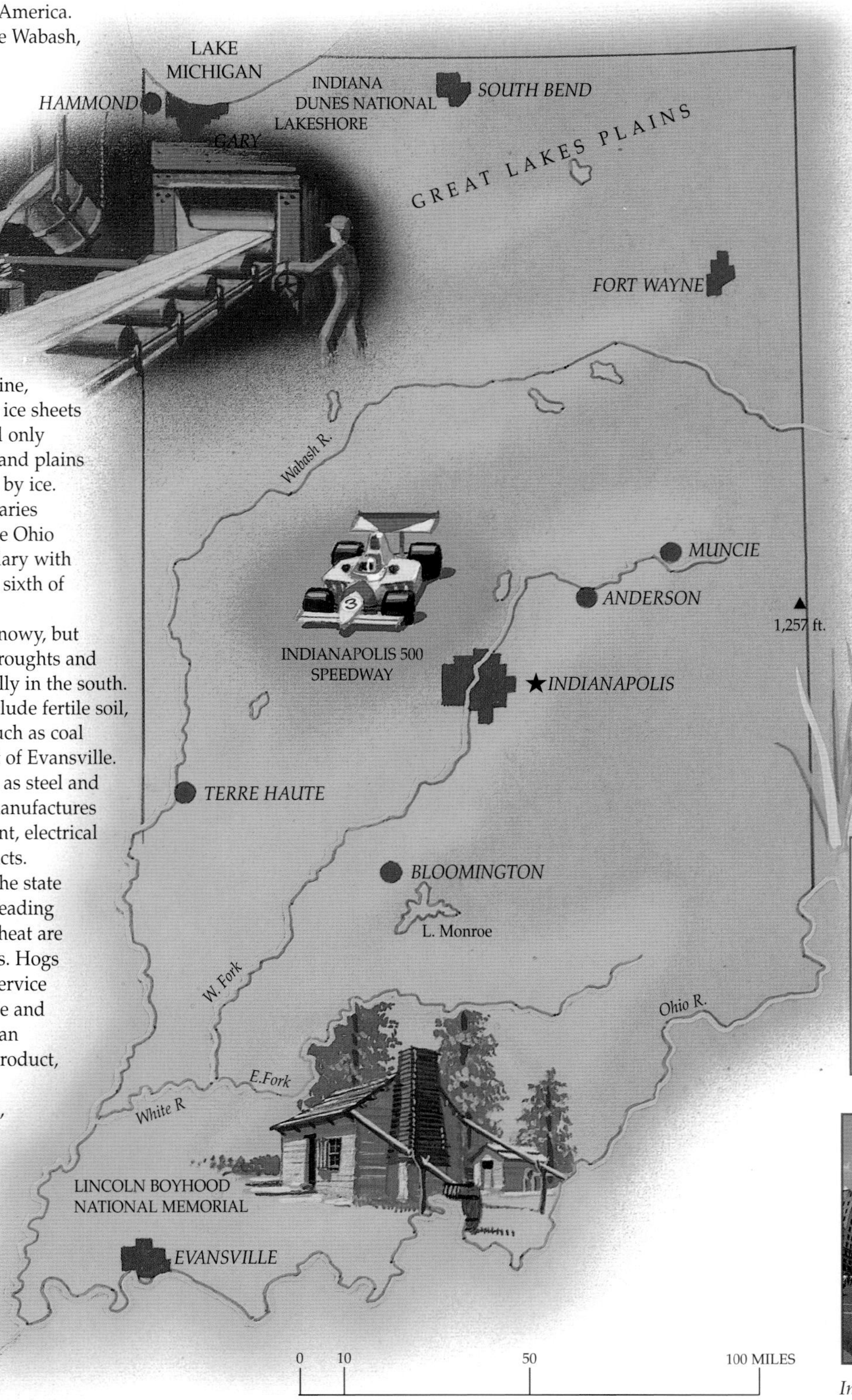
LAKE MICHIGAN
HAMMOND
GARY
INDIANA DUNES NATIONAL LAKESHORE
SOUTH BEND
GREAT LAKES PLAINS
FORT WAYNE
Wabash R.
MUNCIE
ANDERSON
1,257 ft.
INDIANAPOLIS 500 SPEEDWAY
INDIANAPOLIS
TERRE HAUTE
BLOOMINGTON
L. Monroe
W. Fork
Ohio R.
E.Fork
White R
LINCOLN BOYHOOD NATIONAL MEMORIAL
EVANSVILLE
0 10 50 100 MILES

INDIANA

Indianapolis.

Iowa

Iowa, nicknamed the Hawkeye State, probably after a Native American chief named Black Hawk, is also sometimes called the Corn State. One of the Midwestern States, it ranks 25th in area and 30th in population.

Area: 56,275 sq. miles (145,752 sq. km.).
Population (1995): 2,841,764. *Urban:* 59%; *rural:* 49%.
Capital: Des Moines.
Largest cities (1990 census): Des Moines (193,189), Cedar Rapids (108,772), Davenport (95,333), Sioux City (80,505), Waterloo (66,467), Iowa City (59,735), Dubuque (57,538).
State motto: Our Liberties We Prize And Our Rights We Will Maintain.
State song: "The Song of Iowa."
State symbols: *Flower:* wild rose; *bird:* eastern goldfinch; *tree:* oak.
Land features: Iowa forms part of the vast Interior Plains of the United States. Ice sheets covered most of the land during the Ice Age, which ended 10,000 years ago. When they melted, they left behind a layer of moraine, loose rocks and soil over most of the land. The state's highest point, 1,670 ft. (509 m.), lies near its northwest border with Minnesota. Iowa lies between the Mississippi River, which forms the state's eastern border, and the Missouri and Big Sioux rivers, which form the western border. The other rivers in Iowa belong to the Mississippi-Missouri river system. Trees grow in river valleys, but most of the state is open country.
Climate: Cold winters and hot summers are the main features of the climate. Most of the rain falls in spring and summer, but snow is common between January and March.
Economy: Iowa has fertile soils and farming is important. The leading farm product is corn, and Iowa is the nation's leading corn-producing state. Other major crops are soybeans, oats, and hay, while apples and vegetables are also important. Hogs are the main farm animals. The leading manufactures are processed food products, followed by machinery and electrical equipment. However, service industries account for two-thirds of the state's gross product.
Major attractions: DeSoto National Wildlife Refuge, in the Missouri valley, north of Council Bluffs; Effigy Mounds National Monument in the northeast; Herbert Hoover birthplace, West Branch, near Iowa City; Living History Farms, Des Moines.
Famous Iowans: Buffalo Bill Cody, President Herbert C. Hoover, Glenn Miller, James Van Allen, John Wayne, Grant Wood.

KEY DATES

1663 *French explorers Louis Jolliet and Jacques Marquette reached the area.*
1762 *France gave part of its Louisiana colony, including Iowa, to Spain.*
1800 *Spain returned Louisiana to France.*
1803 *The United States gained Iowa as part of the Louisiana Purchase.*
1832 *Native Americans led by Chief Black Hawk were defeated in the Black Hawk War.*
1838 *The Territory of Iowa was created.*
1846 *Iowa became the 29th state.*
1867 *The first railroad was completed across Iowa.*
Mid-1970s *Manufacturing overtook farming as the state's main source of income.*

Rodeo, Iowa.

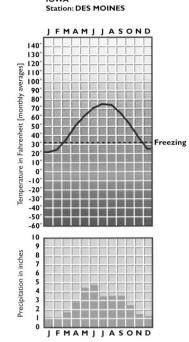

IOWA
Station: DES MOINES

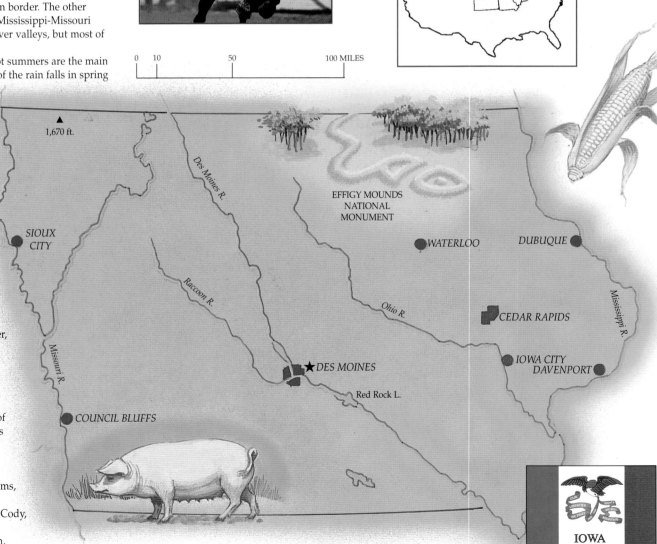

IOWA

50

Kansas

Kansas, the Sunflower State, is also called the Jayhawker State and its people are often called Jayhawkers. Kansas, one of the Midwestern States, ranks 14th in area, but 32nd in population.

Area: 82,277 sq. miles (213,097 sq. km.).
Population (1995): 2,565,328. *Urban:* 67%; *rural:* 33%.
Capital: Topeka.
Largest cities (1990 census): Wichita (304,017), Kansas City (149,800), Topeka (119,883), Overland Park (111,790), Lawrence (65,608).
State motto: *Ad Astra Per Aspera* (To the stars through difficulties).
State song: "Home on the Range."
State symbols: *Flower*: sunflower; *bird*: western meadowlark; *tree*: cottonwood.
Land features: Most of Kansas consists of plains. The land in the east is around 1,500 ft. (around 460 m.) above sea level, but the land slopes upwards to the west to the Great, or High, Plains, where the state's highest point, Mount Sunflower reaches 4,039 ft. (1,231 m.) near the Colorado border. The chief waterways are the Kansas River system in the north and the Arkansas River in the south. The Missouri River forms the state's northeastern border. Trees grow along the rivers, but most of Kansas is former open prairie, which is now largely farmed.
Climate: Kansas has a continental climate, with cold winters and hot summers. The southeast has plenty of rainfall, but to the west it becomes increasingly

dry. The weather is often changeable, with winter blizzards, summer thunderstorms, and tornadoes.
Economy: The state's natural resources include oil, natural gas, and coal, together with fertile soils. Although droughts have caused soil erosion, farming remains important. Beef cattle and wheat are the leading products, followed by grain sorghum, hay, hogs, and corn. Manufacturing is important, especially in the areas around Kansas City and Wichita. Major products include transportation equipment and processed foods. Oil and natural gas are the leading mineral products, but service industries account for around 75% of the state's gross product.
Major attractions: Dodge City-Boot Hill & Frontier Town; Eisenhower Library and Museum, Abilene; Fort Leavenworth; Fort Larned National Historic Site, near Larned; Fort Scott National Historic Site; Kansas Cosmosphere and Space Discovery Center, Hutchinson; U.S. Cavalry Museum, Fort Riley.
Famous Kansans: Walter Chrysler, Amelia Earhart, William Inge, Buster Keaton.

KEY DATES

1541   *The Spaniard Francisco Vásquez de Coronado reached Kansas.*
1803   *The United States took over Kansas as part of the Louisiana Purchase.*
1850s   *Fighting between proslavery and abolitionist groups led the state to be nicknamed "Bleeding Kansas."*
1854   *The Territory of Kansas was created.*
1861   *Kansas became the 34th state.*
1894   *Oil and natural gas production began.*
1934-5   *Droughts cause serious wind erosion and great dust storms.*

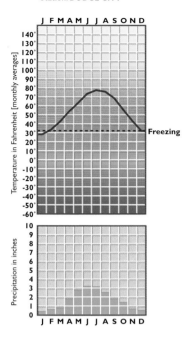

KANSAS
Station: DODGE CITY

Drag meeting at Topeka.

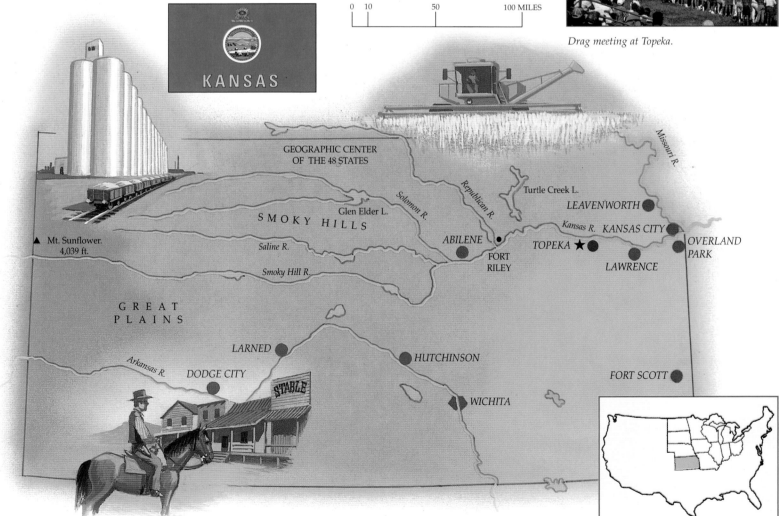

Michigan

Michigan, a Midwestern State, is nicknamed the Wolverine State after the fur pelts brought by early traders. It is the 23rd largest state, but ranks 8th in population.

Area: 97,102 sq. miles (251,493 sq. km.).
Population (1995): 9,549,353. *Urban:* 71%; *rural:* 29%.
Capital: Lansing
Largest cities (1990 census): Detroit (1,027,974), Grand Rapids (189,126), Warren (close to Detroit and not on the map, 144,664), Flint (140,925), Lansing (127,321).
State motto: *Si Quaeris Peninsulam Amoenam Circumspice* (If you seek a pleasant peninsula, look about you).
State song: "Michigan, My Michigan."
State symbols: *Flower:* apple blossom; *bird:* robin; *tree:* white pine.
Land features: Plains bordering three of the Great Lakes make up most of Michigan, but the northwest is composed of upland. This region contains the state's highest point, Mount Curwood, which reaches 1,980 ft. (604 m.). This rugged region contains some rich copper and iron ore deposits. Michigan also includes parts of lakes Huron, Michigan and Superior and the lakes contain several islands, the largest of which is Isle Royale in Lake Superior. Forests cover about half of the state.
Climate: Winters are cold and snowy in Michigan. Summers are warm in the south, but cool in the north. The total precipitation, including rain and snow, varies from around 26 to 36 inches (660-914 mm.).
Economy: Natural resources include fertile soils, forests, and such minerals as iron, copper, oil, and natural gas. The leading manufactures are transport equipment, especially automobiles. Detroit is called "The Automobile Capital of the World," though several other cities in Michigan also make automobiles. Other manufactures include machinery, metal products, chemicals, and processed foods. Farmland covers about a third of the state. Crops include corn, soybeans, and wheat. Fruit and vegetable-growing are also important, while other major farm products include milk, beef cattle, and hogs. However, service industries make up about two-thirds of the state's gross product.
Major attractions: Greenfield Village (historic buildings and Henry Ford Museum), Dearborn, close to Detroit; Isle Royale National Park, in Lake Superior; Pictured Rocks National Lakeshore, on Lake Superior; Sleeping Bear Dunes National Lakeshore, on the northeastern coast of Lake Michigan; Soo Canals, Sault Ste. Marie.

Famous Michiganders: Ralph Bunche, Edna Ferber, Henry Ford, Magic Johnson, Will Kellogg, Ring Lardner, Charles Lindbergh.

KEY DATES

1688 The French explorer Fr. Jacques Marquette founded the first permanent European settlement in Michigan at Sault Ste. Marie.
1763 The British took over what is now Michigan.
1783 Michigan became part of the United States after the end of the Revolutionary War.
1805 The Territory of Michigan was created.
1837 Michigan became the 26th state of the Union.
1855 The Soo Canal was completed, enabling ships to pass between lakes Huron and Superior.
1899 The first automobile plant was opened in Detroit.
1942-5 The automobile industry was turned over to war production during World War II.

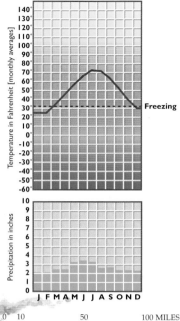

MICHIGAN
Station: DETROIT

Temperature in Fahrenheit [monthly averages]
Freezing

Precipitation in inches

0 10   50   100 MILES

Renaissance Center, Detroit.

ISLE ROYALE NATIONAL PARK

LAKE SUPERIOR

KEWEENAW BAY

Mt. Curwood 1,980 ft.

PICTURED ROCKS NATIONAL LAKESHORE

SAULT STE. MARIE

SOO CANALS

DRUMMOND I.

STRAITS OF MACKINAC

BEAVER I.

GREEN BAY

SLEEPING DUNES NATIONAL LAKESHORE

Manistee R.

Au Sable R.

Muskegon R.

SAGINAW BAY

LAKE HURON

BAY CITY

SAGINAW

MUSKEGON

Grand R.

FLINT

GRAND RAPIDS

★ LANSING

IRISH HILLS

Kalamazoo R.

DETROIT

LAKE ST. CLAIR

KALAMAZOO

JACKSON

ANN ARBOR

LAKE MICHIGAN

LAKE ERIE

Minnesota

Minnesota, nicknamed the Gopher State, is the largest of the Midwestern States. It is the 12th largest, but ranks 20th in population.

Area: 86,614 sq. miles (224,329 sq. km.).
Population (1995): 4,609,548. *Urban:* 67%; *rural:* 33%.
Capital: St. Paul.
Largest cities (1990 census): Minneapolis (368,383), St. Paul (272,235), Bloomington (close to Minneapolis and not shown on the map, 86,335), Duluth (85,493), Rochester (70,729).
State motto: *L'Etoile du Nord* (The Star of the North).
State song: "Hail! Minnesota."
State symbols: *Flower:* pink and white lady's-slipper; *bird:* common loon; *tree:* Norway pine.
Land features: During the Ice Age, which ended only about 10,000 years ago, huge ice sheets covered what is now Minnesota. On the western and southern lowlands, the melting ice sheets dumped soil and rocks over the land, blocking rivers and creating swamps and thousands of lakes. The state's highest point, Eagle Mountain, reaches 2,301 ft. (701 m.) in the Superior Uplands which make up northeastern Minnesota. Important rivers include the Mississippi and its tributary, the Minnesota River. Forests cover just over one-third of the state.
Climate: Minnesota has cold, snowy winters and mild summers. The precipitation (including rain and melted snow) varies from 19 inches (483 mm.) in the northwest to 32 inches (813 mm.) in the southeast.
Economy: The state's natural resources include fertile soils, forests, and iron ore deposits. Farmland covers about half of the area. Milk, beef cattle, and hogs are important products, while major crops include corn, soybeans, hay, and wheat. Fruit (especially apples) and vegetables are also grown. The most important manufactures are machinery, including computers. The state also produces processed food, printed materials, metal products, and scientific instruments. However, service industries account for seven-tenths of the state's gross product.
Major attractions:
Chippewa National Forest, in north-central Minnesota; Grand Portage National Monument, in the northeast; Mayo Clinic, Rochester; Pipestone National Monument, in the southwest; Saint Croix and Lower Saint Croix National Scenic Rivers, both in eastern Minnesota; Superior National Forest, in the northeast; Voyageurs National Park, near the state's northeastern border with Canada.

Famous Minnesotans:
F. Scott Fitzgerald, Judy Garland, Sinclair Lewis.

KEY DATES

1660 *French fur traders reached the area which is now Minnesota.*
1783 *At the end of the Revolutionary War, Britain passed over the land east of the Mississippi River to the United States.*
1803 *The land west of the Mississippi that is now Minnesota was obtained by the United States through the Louisiana Purchase.*
1849 *Minnesota Territory was created.*
1858 *Minnesota became the 32nd state of the Union.*
1862 *A Sioux uprising was put down.*
1889 *The Mayo Clinic was founded in Rochester; it became a major medical research center.*

Winter Carnival, Ice Palace, St. Paul.

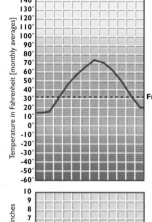

MINNESOTA
Station: **MINNEAPOLIS**

Missouri

Missouri, nicknamed the Show Me State, is one of the 12 Midwestern States. It ranks 19th in area and 16th in population.

Area: 69,697 sq. miles (180,514 sq. km.).
Population (1995): 5,323,523. *Urban:* 68%; *rural:* 32%.
Capital: Jefferson City.
Largest cities (1990 census): Kansas City (434,829), St. Louis (396,685), Springfield (140,494), St. Joseph (71,852), Columbia (69,139).
State motto: *Salus Populi Suprema Lex Esto* (The welfare of the people shall be the supreme law).
State song: "Missouri Waltz."
State symbols: *Flower*: hawthorn; *bird*: bluebird; *tree*: flowering dogwood.
Land features: Northern Missouri consists of plains which are largely covered by soil and rock dumped there by the melting ice sheets at the end of the Ice Age. The Ozark plateau in the south contains the state's highest point, Taum Sauk, which reaches 1,772 ft. (540 m.). The plateau descends in the southeast to the Mississippi flood plain. The Mississippi, which forms the eastern border of the state, and the Missouri, which is the northwestern boundary, are the state's leading rivers. Forests cover about a third of the area.
Climate: Missouri has hot summers and mild winters. The precipitation, including rain and melted snow, varies from 30 inches (762 mm.) in the northwest to 50 inches (1270 mm.) in the southeast.
Economy: The state's natural resources include fertile soils, lead, limestone and coal. Farmland covers about two-thirds of the area and Missouri produces beef cattle, hogs, and turkeys. Dairy farming is also important. Major crops include soybeans, corn, and grain sorghum. Fruits (including apples, peaches, and grapes) and vegetables are also grown. Manufactures include transport equipment, chemicals, and processed food products. However, service industries account for about three-quarters of the state's gross product.
Major attractions:
Gateway Arch, St. Louis;
George Washington Carver National Monument, near Joplin in the southeast;
Lake of the Ozarks, a beautiful recreation area;
Mark Twain House and Museum, Hannibal;
Ulysses S. GrantNational Historic Site, near St. Louis.

Famous Missourians: Omar Bradley, Dale Carnegie. George Washington Carver, T. S. Eliot, Jesse James, President Harry S. Truman, Mark Twain.

KEY DATES

1673   The French explorers Jacques Marquette and Louis Jolliet visited what is now Missouri.
1682   France claimed the area as part of its large colony of Louisiana.
1762   France gave its Louisiana colony to Spain.
1800   Spain returned Louisiana to France.
1803   The United States gained Missouri through the Louisiana Purchase.
1812   The Missouri Territory was established.
1821   Missouri became the 24th state of the Union.
1861-5   Missouri was a battleground during the Civil War.
1945   Harry S. Truman became president of the United States.

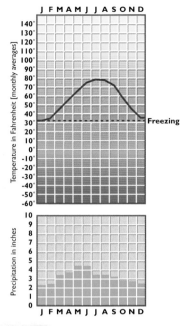

MISSOURI
Station: ST LOUIS

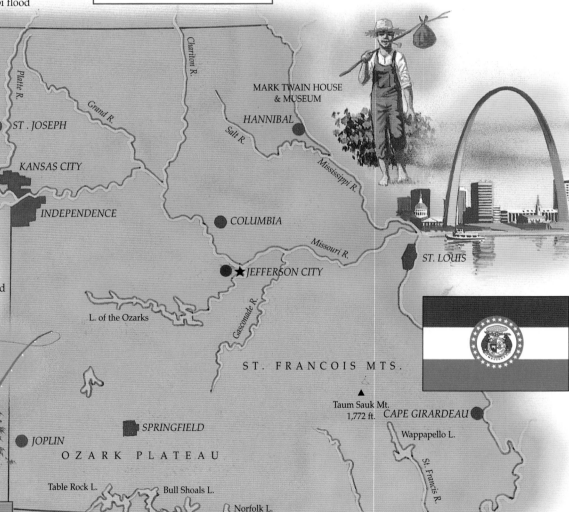

LEFT: Mark Twain's house, Hannibal.

0   10   50   100 MILES

Nebraska

Nebraska, nicknamed the Cornhusker State, is a leading farming state and corn is its chief crop. One of the Midwestern States, it ranks 15th in area, but 37th in population.

Area: 77,355 sq. miles (200,349 sq. km.).
Population (1995): 1,637,112. *Urban: 63%; rural: 37%.*
Capital: Lincoln.
Largest cities (1990 census): Omaha (335,719), Lincoln (191,972), Grand Island (39,487).
State motto: Equality Before the Law.
State song: "Beautiful Nebraska."
State symbols: *Flower*: goldenrod; *bird*: western meadowlark; *tree*: cottonwood.
Land features: Apart from the rolling plains which occupy the eastern fifth of the state, the rest of Nebraska lies in a huge dry region called the Great Plains. The land rises from about 800 ft. (244 m.) in the southeast to a highest point of 5,426 ft. (1,654 m,) in the southwest. A large area of sand dunes, called the Sand Hill Region, occupies central Nebraska. Normally, the loose sand in this region is held together by grasses. The chief rivers are the Niobrara and Platte, which flow into the Missouri River, which forms the state's eastern border. Because the rainfall is low, forests cover only one-fiftieth of the state.
Climate: Nebraska has bitterly cold winters and hot summers. The yearly precipitation (rain, snow, and so on) varies from about 27 inches (686 mm.) in the east to less than 18 inches (457 mm.) in the west.
Economy: Farmers in Nebraska take great care to protect their chief natural resources, namely soil and water. Because of the dry climate, overgrazing and other poor farming methods cause soil erosion, while water is scarce. Nebraska has large cattle ranches and the leading farm animals are beef cattle and hogs. Major crops include

corn, soybeans, hay, grain sorghum, and wheat. Manufacturing is important, especially in Omaha and Lincoln. The leading products include processed foods and electrical equipment. However, service industries account for nearly three-quarters of the state's gross product.
Major attractions: Agate Fossil Beds National Monument, in the northwest; Bellevue, the state's oldest town; Boys Town, near Omaha; Chimney Rock National Historic Site, south of Scottsbluff; Homestead National Monument, in the southeast; Scotts Bluff National Monument, west of Scottsbluff.
Famous Nebraskans: Fred Astaire, Marlon Brando, President Gerald R. Ford, Harold Lloyd, Malcolm X (born Malcolm Little).

KEY DATES

1682 The region was claimed for France by Robert Cavelier, Sieur de la Salle. It became part of a large colony called Louisiana.
1762 France gave the Louisiana colony to Spain.
1800 Spain returned Louisiana to France.
1803 The U.S. purchased Louisiana, including Nebraska.
1843 The "Great Migration" began through Nebraska to the west.
1854 The Nebraska Territory was created.
1865 The Union Pacific Railroad began building a line west from Omaha.
1867 Nebraska became the 37th state of the Union.
1973 Gerald R. Ford became president of the United States.

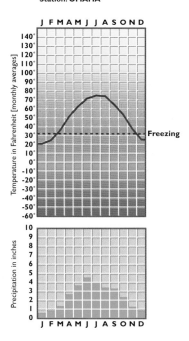

NEBRASKA
Station: OMAHA

Nebraska farm.

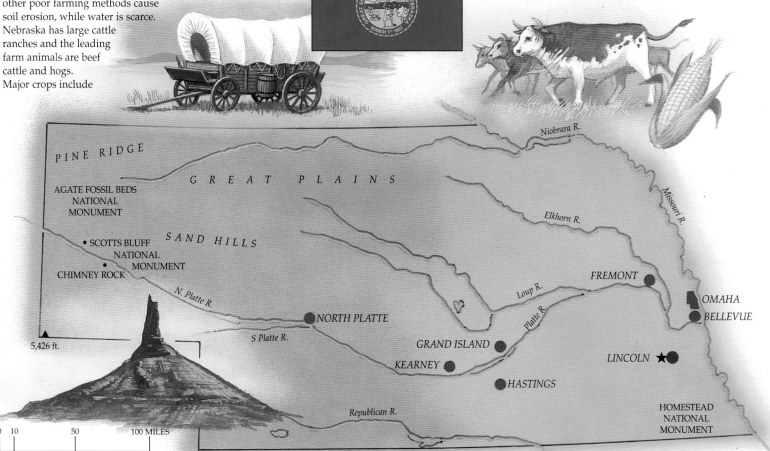

North Dakota

North Dakota, nicknamed the Flickertail State for its flickertail ground squirrels or the Peace Garden State after the International Peace Garden on the Manitoba border, is a Midwestern State. It ranks 17th in area, but ranks 47th in population.

Area: 70,702 sq. miles (183,118 sq. km.).
Population (1995): 641,367. *Urban:* 51%; *rural:* 49%.
Capital: Bismarck.
Largest cities (1990 census): Fargo (74,084), Grand Forks (49,417), Bismarck (49,272), Minot (34,544).
State motto: Liberty and Union, Now and Forever, One and Inseparable.
State song: "North Dakota Hymn."
State symbols: *Flower:* wild prairie rose; *bird:* western meadowlark; *tree:* American elm.
Land features: The land in North Dakota rises from the Red River valley in the east, through a higher region of prairie which extends from the northwest to the southeast, and then to the high Great Plains in the southwest. The state's highest point, White Butte, reaches 3,506 ft. (1,069 m.) in the scenic Badlands in the southwest. The main rivers are the Missouri, which crosses the Great Plains region, the James River, which rises in central North Dakota, and the Red River which forms the state's eastern border. Forests cover only about 1% of this dry state.
Climate: North Dakota has warm summers and cold winters when bitterly cold winds sometimes make conditions extremely unpleasant. The precipitation, including rain and melted snow, decreases from the northeast to the southwest, which is semidesert.
Economy: The state's chief resources are its fertile soils and its deposits of oil, natural gas, and coal. Agriculture is the leading activity. The major crops are wheat, barley, sunflower seeds, hay, and flaxseed. Corn, honey, oats, potatoes, rye, and sugar beets are also produced. Beef and dairy cattle are also raised. Mining and manufacturing contribute about 12% of the state's gross product. Oil is the chief mineral, while manufactures include processed food products and machinery. However, service industries account for seven-tenths of the state's gross product.
Major attractions: Fort Union Trading Post National Historic Site, near Williston; International Peace Garden, which extends into Manitoba; Knife River Indian Villages National Historic Site, near Bismarck; Theodore Roosevelt National Park, in the Badlands region.
Famous North Dakotans: Carl Ben Eielson, Louis L'Amour.

KEY DATES

1682 Southwestern North Dakota was part of a huge area claimed by France.
1803 The United States took southwestern North Dakota as part of the Louisiana Purchase.
1818 The United States took over northeastern North Dakota following an agreement with Britain.
1861 The Dakota Territory was created.
1873 The Northern Pacific Railroad reached Bismarck.
1889 North Dakota became the 39th state of the Union.
1951 Oil was discovered in the northeast.

**NORTH DAKOTA
Station: WILLISTON**

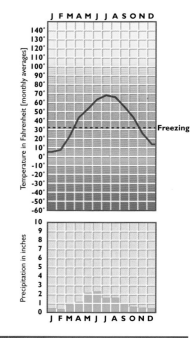

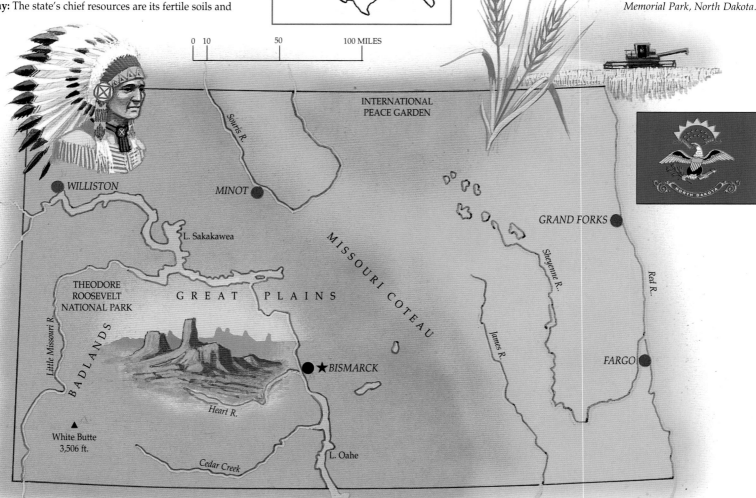

Theodore Roosevelt National Memorial Park, North Dakota.

56

Ohio

Ohio, which was named the Buckeye State after the many buckeye trees which once grew there, is the most easterly of the Midwestern States. Although it is only the 37th state in area, it ranks 7th in population.

Area: 44,787 sq. miles (115,998 sq. km.).
Population (1995): 11,150,506. *Urban*: 73%; *rural*: 27%.
Capital: Columbus.
Largest cities (1990 census): Columbus (632,945), Cleveland (505,616), Cincinnati (364,114), Toledo (332,943), Akron (223,019), Dayton (182,005).
State motto: With God, All Things Are Possible.
State song: "Beautiful Ohio."
State symbols: *Flower*: scarlet carnation; *bird*: cardinal; *tree*: buckeye.
Land features: From the Great Lakes Plains facing Lake Erie in the north, the land rises to the Allegheney Plateau in the southeast and the plains of the southwest. The southwestern plains are largely covered by soil and rock dumped there by ice sheets at the end of the Ice Age. The state's highest point, Campbell Hill in west-central Ohio, reaches 1,550 ft. (472 m.). Ohio's main rivers are the Ohio, which forms the state's southern border, and its tributaries. Forests cover about a quarter of the land.
Climate: Ohio has warm summers and cold, snowy winters. Precipitation, including rain and melted snow, occurs throughout the year.
Economy: Ohio's chief natural resources include fertile soils, coal, oil, and natural gas. The major crops are corn and soybeans, and milk is also important. Farm animals include beef cattle, hogs, poultry, and sheep. Fruit and vegetables are also leading products. Coal is mined, but the state's most valuable activity is manufacturing. Manufactures include transportation equipment (including motor vehicles and parts for motor vehicles) and airplanes. Ohio also produces machinery, metal products, chemicals, and metals, especially steel. However, service industries account for seven-tenths of the state's gross product.
Major attractions:
Air Force Museum, Dayton; Cuyahoga Valley National Recreation Area, between Akron and Cleveland; Great Serpent Mound; Neil Armstrong Air and Space Museum, Fremont, southeast of Toledo; Perry's Victory and International Peace Memorial, South Bass Island, Lake Erie; Rutherford B. Hayes National Historic Site, Cincinnati.
Famous Ohioans: Six Presidents were born in Ohio. They were James A. Garfield, Ulysses S. Grant, Benjamin Harrison, Rutherford B. Hayes, William McKinley, and William H. Taft. Other Ohioans include Neil Armstrong, Thomas Edison, John Glenn, William Sherman, James Thurber, and Orville and Wilbur Wright.

KEY DATES

1670   René-Robert Cavelier, Sieur de La Salle, a French explorer, probably reached Ohio.
1763   Britain took over the Ohio region from France.
1803   Ohio (formerly called the Northwest Territory) became the 17th state of the Union.
1832   The Ohio and Erie Canal was completed, increasing trade in the area.
1872   A rubber industry was founded in Akron.
1980s Efforts were made to clean up pollution in Lake Erie and Ohio's rivers.

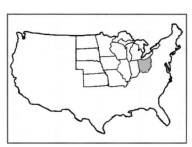

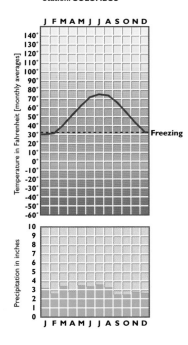

OHIO
Station: **COLUMBUS**

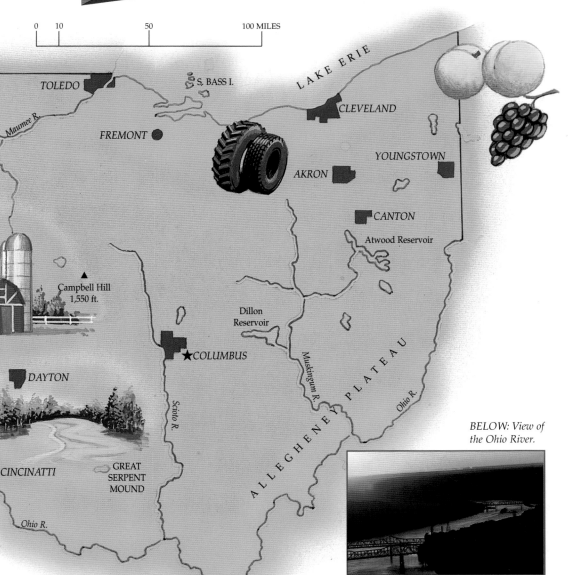

0   10   50   100 MILES

BELOW: View of the Ohio River.

South Dakota

South Dakota, one of the Midwestern States, is nicknamed the Sunshine State. It is the 16th largest state, but ranks 45th in population.

Area: 77,116 sq. miles (199,730 sq. km.).
Population (1995): 729,034. *Urban:* 54%; *rural:* 46%.
Capital: Pierre.
Largest cities (1990 census): Sioux Falls (100,836), Rapid City (54,523), Aberdeen (24,995).
State motto: Under God the People Rule.
State song: "Hail South Dakota."
State symbols: *Flower:* American pasqueflower; *bird:* ring-necked pheasant; *tree:* Black Hills spruce.
Land features: From a region of low hills and prairie in the east, the land rises to the largely treeless Great Plains, which cover about two-thirds of the state. Parts of the Great Plains have been worn into badlands, especially to the southeast of the Black Hills, a mountainous region in the far west. The Black Hills contain the state's highest point, Harney Peak, which reaches 7,242 ft. (2,707 m.). The chief river is the Missouri, whose valley contains four lakes which have formed behind dams. Forests cover only about 4% of the land, occurring mainly in the Black Hills.
Climate: North Dakota has hot summers and cold winters. The precipitation, including rain and melted snow, ranges from about 25 inches (635 mm.) in the southeast to 13 inches (330 mm.) in the northwest. The wettest months are April through to August.
Economy: The state's natural resources include fertile soils and minerals, such as gold. About half of the state is grazing land, where farmers raise beef cattle, hogs, and sheep. The main crops are corn, wheat, and sunflowers. Flaxseed, grain sorghum, hay, oats, and rye are also grown. Food processing is the chief industry. Other manufactures include machinery, scientific instruments, and electrical and electronic equipment. However, service industries account for about seven-tenths of the state's gross product.
Major attractions: Badlands National Park, east of Rapid City; Crazy Horse Memorial; Deadwood, the Old West town in the Black Hills, northwest of Rapid City; Jewel Cave National Monument, southwest of Rapid City; Mount Rushmore National Memorial, southwest of Rapid City; Wind Cave National Park, south of Rapid City.
Famous South Dakotans: Crazy Horse, Ernest O. Lawrence, Sitting Bull.

KEY DATES

1682 René-Robert Cavelier, Sieur de la Salle, claimed for France the huge colony of Louisiana, which contained what is now South Dakota.
1803 South Dakota became part of the United States through the Louisiana Purchase.
1861 The Dakota Territory was created.
1874 Gold was discovered in the Black Hills.
1889 South Dakota became the 40th state of the Union.
1890 Federal troops massacred Sioux Indians at Wounded Knee.
1927 The sculptor Gutzon Borglum started work on the Mount Rushmore National Monument; it was completed in 1941.
1930s Droughts caused soil erosion in South Dakota.
1973 A group of Native Americans occupied the village of Wounded Knee in a protest against federal policies.

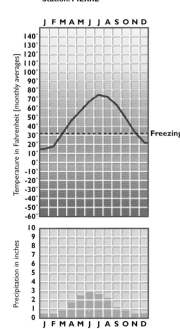

SOUTH DAKOTA
Station: PIERRE

Buffalo ranch, South Dakota.

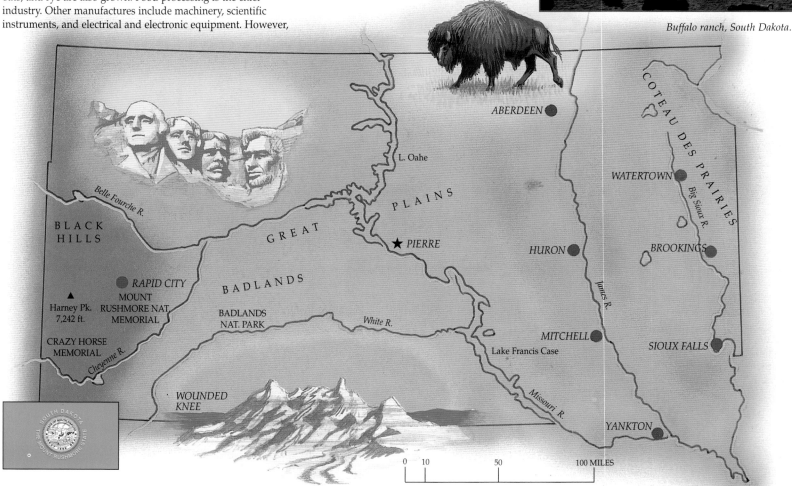

Wisconsin

Wisconsin is one of the Midwestern States. Nicknamed the Badger State after the name given to its miners in the early 19th century, Wisconsin is the 26th largest state and ranks 18th in population.

Area: 66,215 sq. miles (171,496 sq. km.).
Population: (1995): 5,122,871. *Urban*: 64%; *rural*: 36%.
Capital: Madison.
Largest cities: Milwaukee (628,088), Madison (190,766), Green Bay (96,466), Racine (84,298), Kenosha (80,426).
State motto: Forward.
State song: "On, Wisconsin."
State symbols: *Flower*: wood violet; *bird*: robin; *tree*: sugar maple.
Land features: Wisconsin, which has shorelines on Lake Superior in the north and Lake Michigan in the southeast, has highly varied scenery, with many lakes, fertile lowlands, and uplands in the the north and southwest. The highest point is Timms Hill, which reaches 1,952 ft. (595 m.) in the north. Much of the scenery of Wisconsin was shaped by ice sheets during the last Ice Age, which ended only about 10,000 years ago. The ice sheets wore down many upland areas and dumped the worn soil and rock on the lowlands, blocking rivers and forming lakes. Many of the state's

rivers flow into the Mississippi (above), which forms much of its western border. Forests cover about half of the land.
Climate: Most of Wisconsin has long, cold winters and short, warm summers, though the plains along the lakeshores have a milder climate than the interior. The average yearly precipitation, including rain and melted snow, is around 30 inches (762 mm.).
Economy: The state's natural resources include fertile soils, plentiful water supplies, forests, and building stone. Dairy farming is important, and milk is a major product. Farmers also raise beef cattle and hogs, while the leading crops are corn and hay. Other crops include barley,

oats, soybeans, tobacco, and wheat. Fruits and vegetables are also grown. Manufactures include machinery, processed food products (including butter and cheese), paper and metal products. However, service industries account for about two-thirds of the state's gross product.
Major attractions: Apostle Islands National Lakeshore in Lake Superior; Saint Croix National Scenic River, which Wisconsin shares with Minnesota.
Famous Wisconsinites: Joseph R. McCarthy, Spencer Tracy. Orson Welles, Thornton Wilder, Frank Lloyd Wright.

KEY DATES

1634 *A French explorer, Jean Nicolet, reached what is now Wisconsin.*
1763 *England took control of Wisconsin from France.*
1783 *Wisconsin became part of the United States.*
1832 *The Native Americans were defeated in the Black Hawk War.*
1838 *Wisconsin Territory was created.*
1848 *Wisconsin became the 30th state of the Union.*

WISCONSIN
Station: MILWAUKEE

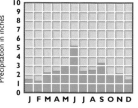

0   10   50   100 MILES

WISCONSIN
1848

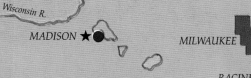

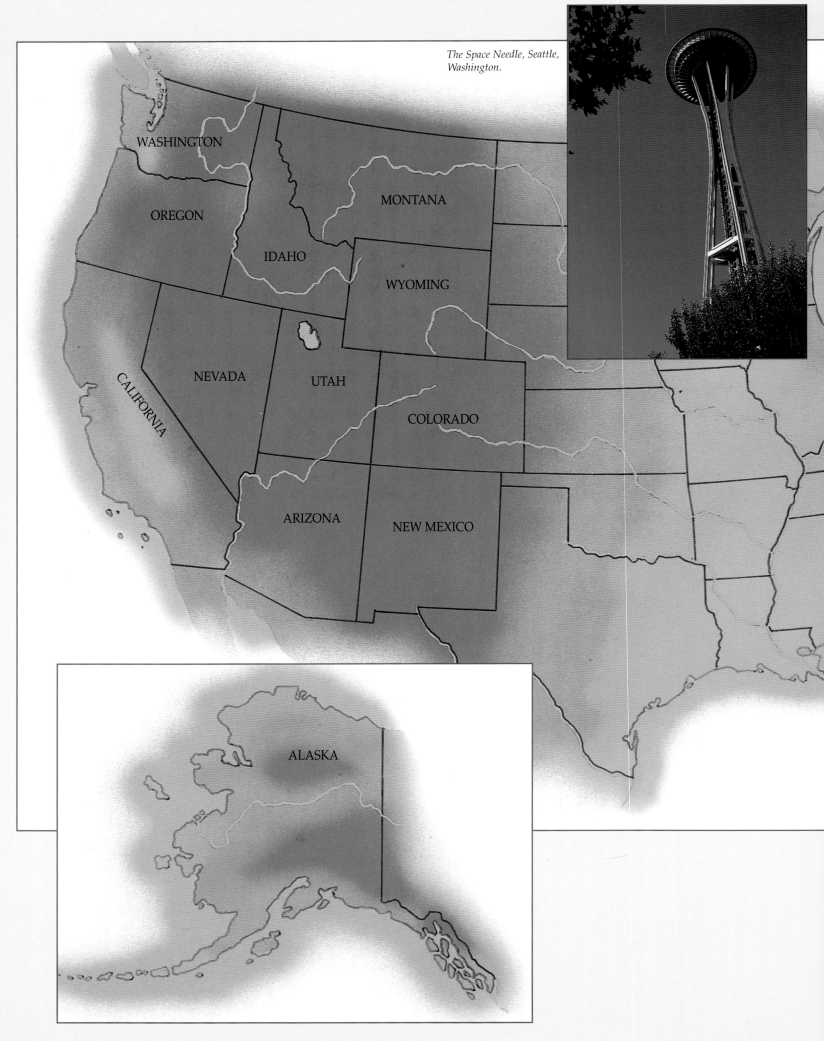

The Space Needle, Seattle, Washington.

WASHINGTON

OREGON

IDAHO

MONTANA

WYOMING

NEVADA

UTAH

CALIFORNIA

COLORADO

ARIZONA

NEW MEXICO

ALASKA

Western and Mountain States

Glacier National Park,
McDonald Creek, Montana.

The six Rocky Mountain states, the three Pacific Coast states, together with the southwestern states of Arizona and New Mexico, contain much of the world's most spectacular scenery. Together with the two detached states of Alaska and Hawaii, the group contains nearly two-thirds of the country's 54 national parks, Alaska alone having eight, California six, and Utah five.

The towering Rocky Mountains are the greatest range in North America. They extend from New Mexico, north through Colorado, Utah, Wyoming, Idaho, Montana, and Washington, through Canada, into northern Alaska. West of the Rockies lies a region of basins – formed when blocks of land sank down between huge faults (fractures) in the Earth's crust – uplifted ranges, and vast plateaus. One of the basins is Death Valley, a fiercely hot desert, while the Sierra Nevada in California is an uplifted mountain range. The lava-covered Columbia plateau is in the north, while the arid Colorado plateau is crossed by the Colorado River, which has worn out the amazing Grand Canyon in northern Arizona.

The Cascade Range in Oregon and Washington contains active volcanoes, while the land along the San Andreas fault in California is periodically hit by devastating earthquakes. Other regions of great instability are southern Alaska and the huge volcanoes of Big Island, Hawaii which discharge rivers of lava into the sea.

The region includes huge cities, including the sprawling Los Angeles, the nation's second largest. Also among the nation's 25 largest cities are San Diego, California, a port near the border with Mexico; San Jose, California, which is famed for its high-tech industries; Phoenix, Arizona, one of the nation's fastest growing cities; San Francisco, California, a magnificent city and a great cultural center; Seattle, Washington, a major economic center; and Denver, Colorado, the "Mile High City," whose beautiful backdrop is formed by the frontal ranges of the Rocky Mountains.

Alaska

Unofficially called "The Last Frontier," Alaska is the largest state though ranking 48th in population. Purchased from Russia in 1867 by Secretary of State William H. Seward, it was often known as "Seward's Folly," but it proved to be rich in oil, timber, and fish.

Area: 591,004 sq. miles (1,530,693 sq. km.).
Population (1995): 603,617. *Urban:* 64%; *rural:* 36%.
Capital: Juneau.
Largest cities (1990 census): Anchorage (226,338), Fairbanks (30,843), Juneau (26,751).
State motto: North to the Future.
State song: "Alaska's Flag."
State symbols: *Flower:* forget-me-not; *bird:* willow ptarmigan; *tree:* Sitka spruce.
Land features: Southern Alaska is mountainous and the Alaska Range includes the highest point in North America, Mount McKinley, at 20,320 ft. (6,194 m.). Central Alaska contains hills and swampy valleys, drained by the Yukon and other rivers. To the north, the Brooks Range overlooks the Arctic coastal plain. Volcanic eruptions and earthquakes are common in the south and in the Aleutian Islands which stretch to the southwest. Forests cover about a third of the land, though the north is too cold for trees. Large areas of highlands, especially in the south and southeast, are covered by glaciers.
Climate: Southern Alaska has mild summers, but winters are cold. The interior and the north have much harsher climates, with bitterly cold winters and short summers.
Economy: The chief resources are oil and natural gas and Alaska also has gold and other metal deposits. Fishing, the processing of fish products, and forestry are other important activities, but farming is limited by the short growing season. Service industries, including tourism, account for about half the state's gross product.
Major attractions: National parks include Denali, which contains Mount McKinley; Gates of the Arctic; Katmai; Kenai Fjords; Kobuk Valley; Lake Clark; and Wrangell-St. Elias. The state also contains the Klondike Gold Rush and the Sitka National Historical Parks.

ALASKA
Station: ANCHORAGE

ALASKA
Station: BARROW

KEY DATES

1741 The Danish explorer Vitus Bering, sailing for Russia, landed on Alaskan islands.
1784 The Russians set up the first European settlement on Kodiak Island.
1867 Russia sold Alaska to the United States for $7.2 million – or about 2 cents per acre.
1897-8 The discovery of gold led to the Klondike and Alaska gold rush.
1912 Alaska became a U.S. territory.
1942 Japan invaded two of the Aleutian Islands; the Alaska Highway was completed, linking the area to American states and to Canada.
1959 Alaska became the 49th state.
1964 A severe earthquake caused great damage around Anchorage and Valdez.
1968 A huge oilfield was discovered on Alaska's Arctic plain.
1980 The work of conservationists led to about 25% of the state being placed under the National Park system.
1989 The oil tanker Exxon Valdez ran aground and caused a huge oil spill. Much damage was done.

ARCTIC OCEAN

BARROW

BERING STRAIT

GATES OF THE ARCTIC NATIONAL PARK

KOBUK VALLEY NATIONAL PARK

BROOKS RANGE

ARCTIC CIRCLE

Porcupine R.

NOME

ST. LAWRENCE I.

Yukon R.

FAIRBANKS

Tanana R.

BERING SEA

ALASKA RANGE

Mt. McKinley 20,320 ft.

Kuskokwim R.

TRANS ALASKA PIPELINE

NUNIVAK I.

MENDENHALL GLACIER

ANCHORAGE

KENAI

KATMAI NATIONAL PARK

KENAI FJORDS NATIONAL PARK

GULF OF ALASKA

KODIAK

ALEUTIAN IS.

KODIAK I.

JUNEAU

SITKA

KETCHIKAN

RIGHT:
Chiswell Islands.

0 50 100 200 400 MILES

Arizona

Arizona, one of the Southwestern States, is called the Grand Canyon State. Known for its sunshine and scenery, it is the 6th largest state, ranking 23rd in population.

Area: 114,000 sq. miles (295,259 sq. km.).
Population (1995): 4,217,940. *Urban:* 84%; *rural:* 16%.
Capital: Phoenix.
Largest cities (1990 census): Phoenix (983,403), Tucson (405,323). Other cities which lie close to Phoenix and do not appear on the map are Mesa (288,104), Glendale (147,864), Tempe (141,993), and Scottsdale (130,075).
State motto: *Ditat Deus* (God enriches).
State songs: "Arizona."
State symbols: *Flower*: saguaro; *bird*: cactus wren; *tree*: paloverde.
Land features: The Colorado River, the state's main waterway, has worn out the magnificent Grand Canyon in the Colorado Plateau, which covers most of northern Arizona. Rising above the plateau near Flagstaff is the state's highest point, Humphreys Peak, at 12,633 ft. (3,851 m.). Southern Arizona, the basin and range region, contains mountain ranges separated by broad valleys. The state has many artificial lakes created by dams built across the rivers. They include Lake Mead behind the Hoover Dam and Lake Powell, which extends into Utah, behind the Glen Canyon Dam. Forests cover more than 25% of the land.
Climate: Much of Arizona has a desert climate, but mountain areas are much wetter. Temperatures are high in lowlying areas, but winters are bitterly cold in the mountains.
Economy: Service industries, including tourism and facilities provided for the many retired people who have settled in the state, account for nearly four-fifths of Arizona's gross state product. Manufacturing includes high technology industries, producing such things as computers. Much of Arizona is too dry for farming, but beef, cotton, and milk are important products. Copper and gold are mined,
Major attractions: Grand Canyon National Park; London Bridge, Lake Havasu City; Meteor Crater; Montezuma Castle; Monument Valley; Painted Desert; Petrified Forest National Park; Saguaro National Park; the Western town of Tombstone.
Famous Arizonans: Cochise, Barry Goldwater, Carl Hayden.

KEY DATES

1540 The Spanish explorer Francisco Vásquez de Coronado, searched for treasure in Arizona.
1752 Spanish troops founded the first white settlement in the area.
1821 The territory that is now Arizona became part of Mexico when that country won its independence from Spain.
1848 Most of what is now Arizona was taken by the United States at the end of the Mexican War (1846-48).
1863 The Arizona Territory was created.
1886 Geronimo and his Apache force surrendered to U.S. troops.
1912 Arizona became the 48th state of the United States.
1936 The Hoover Dam was completed.
1950s- Arizona's population
1990s increased from about 750,000 in 1950 to 3,670,000 in 1990, as people from other states, attracted by the warm climate, settled in Arizona.

ARIZONA
Station: PHOENIX

J F M A M J J A S O N D

Temperature in Fahrenheit [monthly averages]
140°
130°
120°
110°
100°
90°
80°
70°
60°
50°
40°
30° .... Freezing
20°
10°
0°
-10°
-20°
-30°
-40°
-50°
-60°

Precipitation in inches
10
9
8
7
6
5
4
3
2
1
0

J F M A M J J A S O N D

L. Powell
GLEN CANYON DAM
MONUMENT VALLEY
COLORADO PLATEAU
GRAND CANYON NATIONAL PARK
Colorado R.
L. Mead
HOOVER DAM
L. Mohave
Little Colorado R.
P A I N T E D   D E S E R T
Humphrey's Peak 12,633 ft. ▲
FLAGSTAFF ●
METEOR CRATER
PETRIFIED FOREST NATIONAL PARK
Havasu L.
MONTEZUMA CASTLE NATIONAL MONUMENT
PRESCOTT ●
LONDON BRIDGE
Verde R.
Colorado R.
GILA MTS.
Salt R.
★ PHOENIX
San Carlos L.
Gila R.
Gila R.
S O N O R A N   D E S E R T
YUMA ●
TUCSON ●
TOMBSTONE ●

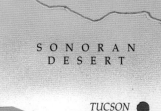
Monument Valley.

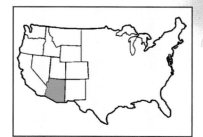

0 10   50   100 MILES

California

California, nicknamed the Golden State after the gold rush of 1849, ranks third in area among the states, but, since 1963, its population has exceeded that of any other state. It is one of the Pacific Coast States.

Area: 158,706 sq. miles (411,049 sq. km.).
Population (1995): 31,589,153. *Urban:* 91%; *rural:* 9%.
Capital: Sacramento.
Largest cities (1990 census): Los Angeles (3,485,557), San Diego (1,110,554), San Jose (782,248), San Francisco (723,959), Long Beach (429,321), Oakland (372,242), Sacramento (369,365), Fresno (354,091).
State motto: *Eureka* (I have found it).
State song: "I Love You, California."
State symbols: *Flower:* golden poppy; *bird:* California valley quail; *tree:* California redwood.
Land features: Mountain ranges include the Sierra Nevada, where the state's highest point, Mount Whitney, reaches 14,495 ft. (4,418 m.), the Klamath and Cascade mountains in the north, and the Los Angeles and San Diego ranges in the south. The fertile Central Valley is drained by the Sacramento and San Joaquin, California's longest rivers. The Mojave Desert is in the southeast, while Death Valley contains the lowest point in the U.S. at 282 ft. (86 m.) below sea level. The San Andreas Fault in the southwest is the boundary between the North American and Pacific plates. Earthquakes are common in this area.
Climate: Southeast California is hot and dry. Death Valley holds the record highest temperature in the United States – 134°F (57°C). The coast has warm, dry summers and mild, moist winters. The mountains are much cooler and snowy.
Economy: California's resources include forests, which cover two-fifths of the land, and such minerals as oil and natural gas. Manufactures include transportation equipment, machinery (including computers made in "Silicon Valley" in the San Jose-Palo Alto area), and food processing. Although southern California suffers from water shortages, farming is important. Milk and beef are major products, while crops include citrus and other fruits, cotton, grapes and vegetables. However, service industries account for 75% of the state's gross product. Experts estimate that if California were a separate country, it would rank among the world's top ten economic powers.
Major attractions: National parks include the Channel Islands, Death Valley, Joshua Tree, Kings Canyon, Lassen Volcanic, Redwood, Sequoia, and Yosemite. Amusement parks include Disneyland at Anaheim and Knott's Berry Farm. Hollywood in Los Angeles is a popular tourist area.
Famous Californians: William R. Hearst, Jack London, Richard Nixon, William Saroyan, John Steinbeck.

KEY DATES

1542 *A Portuguese explorer, sailing from Mexico, reached San Diego Bay.*
1579 *Francis Drake claimed the area for England.*
1769 *The Spanish began to establish settlements and missions in California.*
1822 *California became part of Mexico.*
1848 *Following the Mexican War (1846-48), Mexico dropped its claim to California.*
1849 *The California gold rush began.*
1850 *California became the 31st state.*
1906 *An earthquake destroyed much of San Francisco.*
1989 *An earth tremor rocked the San Francisco area.*

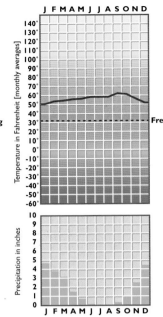

CALIFORNIA
Station: LOS ANGELES

CALIFORNIA
Station: SAN FRANCISCO

Joshua tree in flower.

CALIFORNIA REPUBLIC

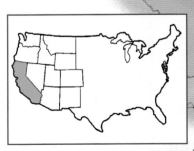

HOLLYWOOD

0 10   50   100   200 MILES

Colorado

Colorado, a Rocky Mountain State, is nicknamed the Centennial State because it joined the Union in 1876, the 100th anniversary of the Declaration of Independence. It is the 8th largest state, though it ranks 25th in population.

Area: 104,091 sq. miles (269,596 sq. km.).
Population (1995): 3,746,585. *Urban:* 81%; *rural:* 19%.
Capital: Denver.
Largest cities (1990 census): Denver (467,610), Colorado Springs (280,430).
State motto: *Nil Sine Numine* (Nothing without providence).
State song: "Where the Columbines Grow."
State symbols: *Flower:* Rocky Mountain columbine; *bird:* lark bunting; *tree:* blue spruce.
Land features: The gently sloping and mostly treeless Great Plains cover eastern Colorado. Denver, which is overlooked by the Rockies, is called "Mile High City" because it is about 1 mile (1.6 km.) above sea level. The Rocky Mountain ranges run north-south through the state. They contain Mount Elbert which, at 14,443 ft. (4,399 m.), is the highest peak in Colorado and in the entire Rocky Mountains. The Colorado Plateau in the west is a region of hills, plateaus and valleys. Many major rivers, including the Arkansas, Colorado, South Platte, and Rio Grande, rise in the state. Forests cover about a third of the land.
Climate: Eastern Colorado has sunny summers and cool winters, but the mountains are much colder.

The Great Plains are sometimes affected by a warm wind, called the chinook, which blows down from the mountains. The Great Plains have an average annual rainfall of about 15 inches (381 mm.), but the wettest areas are the western slopes of the mountains. Snowfalls are important for the winter sports resorts in the Rockies.
Economy: Natural resources include minerals, such as oil and natural gas, gold and coal. Manufactures include scientific instruments, processed farm products, machinery (including computers), metal products and electrical equipment. Beef, lamb and milk are important, while major crops include corn, hay and wheat. However, service industries account for about four-fifths of the state's gross product.
Major attractions: Buffalo Bill's Grave; Garden of the Gods, near Colorado Springs; Dinosaur National Monument; Mesa Verde, Great Sand Dunes, and Rocky Mountains national parks.
Famous Coloradans: Jack Dempsey, Douglas Fairbanks Sr., Paul Whiteman.

KEY DATES

1682 *France claimed eastern Colorado.*
1706 *Spain claimed the area that is now Colorado.*
1803 *The United States purchased east and central Colorado as part of the Louisiana Purchase.*
1848 *The United States took western Colorado after the Mexican War (1846-48).*
1861 *Colorado Territory was created.*
1876 *Colorado became the 38th state.*
1906 *The U.S. Mint in Denver produced its first coins.*
1956 *Work began on the Colorado River Storage Project.*
1958 *The U.S. Air Force Academy was founded at Colorado Springs.*
1972 *The Frying Pan-Arkansas Project, to transfer water from western Colorado to the east, began operating. It was completed in 1985.*

COLORADO
Station: DENVER

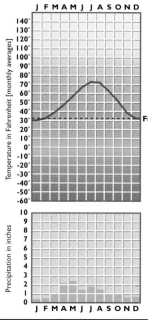

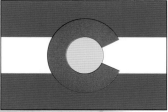

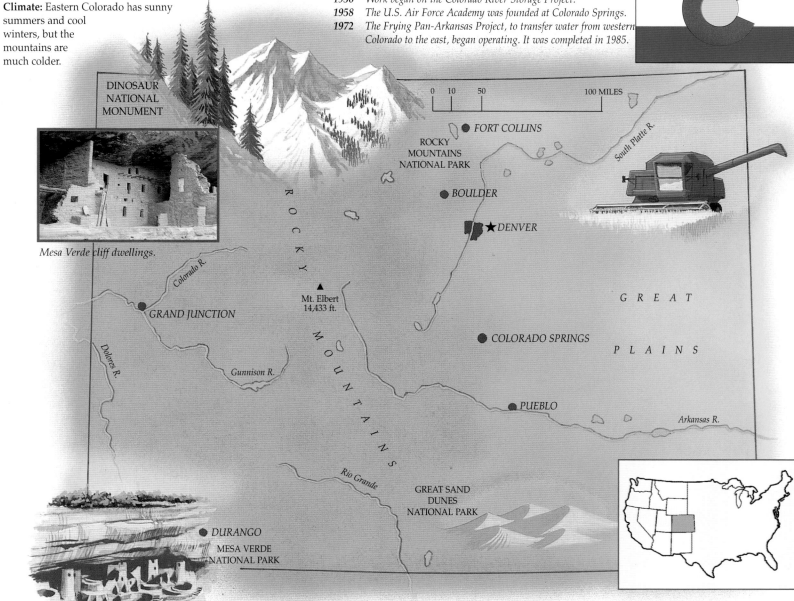

DINOSAUR NATIONAL MONUMENT

Mesa Verde cliff dwellings.

FORT COLLINS
ROCKY MOUNTAINS NATIONAL PARK
BOULDER
★DENVER
South Platte R.

GRAND JUNCTION
Colorado R.
▲ Mt. Elbert 14,433 ft.
Dolores R.
Gunnison R.

COLORADO SPRINGS

G R E A T
P L A I N S

PUEBLO
Arkansas R.

Rio Grande
GREAT SAND DUNES NATIONAL PARK

DURANGO
MESA VERDE NATIONAL PARK

R O C K Y   M O U N T A I N S

0   10   50   100 MILES

California coast between Carmel and Gorda.

Hawaii

Hawaii, the Aloha State, is an island chain in the North Pacific Ocean. It was admitted to the Union as the 50th state in 1959. It ranks 47th in area and 40th in population.

Area: 6,471 sq. miles (16,760 sq. km.).
Population (1995): 1,186,815. *Urban:* 87%; *rural:* 13%.
Capital: Honolulu.
Largest cities (1990 census): Honolulu (365,272), Hilo (37,808), Kailua (36,818).
State motto: *Ua Mau Ke Ea O Ka Aino I Ka Pono* (The life of the land is perpetuated in righteousness).
State song: *Hawaii Ponoi* ("Hawaii's Own").
State symbols: *Flower:* yellow hibiscus; *bird:* nene (Hawaiian goose); *tree:* kukui.
Land features: Hawaii consists of 132 islands. The largest, which is also called Hawaii, has active volcanoes, including Mauna Loa and Kilauea. Mauna Kea, an extinct volcano on Hawaii, is the state's highest peak at 13,796 ft. (4,205 m.). From its base on the sea floor, it rises 33,480 ft. (10,205 m.) high, which would make it the world's tallest mountain. The other large islands extending northwest of Hawaii are Maui, Kahoolawe, Molokai, Lanai, Oahu, where Honolulu is located, Kauai, and Niihau.

Climate: Hawaii is warm throughout the year. The rainfall is generally heaviest on the northeast parts of the islands and on the mountains. Mount Waialeale on Kauai has around 350 rainy days every year.
Economy: Every year, more than 6 million tourists visit the state, especially Oahu, and service industries, especially those that cater for tourists, account for nearly nine-tenths of the state's gross product. Hawaii once depended on the cultivation of sugar cane and pineapples and these crops are still the main ones. Cattle are raised on Hawaii, while dairy products, eggs, and hogs are important on other islands. Fishing, including fish farming, is another major activity. Manufactured products include processed foods, printed materials, oil, clothing, and chemicals.
Major attractions: Haleakala National Park, Maui; Hawaii Volcanoes National Park, Hawaii Island; Kaloko-Honokohau National Historical Park, Oahu;

Kalaupapa National Historical Park, Molokai; Pearl Harbor, Oahu; Polynesian Cultural Center, Oahu; Pu'uhonua o Honaunau National Historical Park; Waikiki Beach, Oahu; Waimea Canyon, Kauai.
Famous Hawaiians: King Kamehameha I, Lydia Kamekeha Liliuokalani (queen of Hawaii, 1891-3).

KEY DATES

1778 *The British Captain James Cook landed on Hawaii,*
1795 *King Kamehameha I unified the islands.*
1820 *New England missionaries arrived and converted most Hawaiians to Christianity.*
1835 *The first permanent sugar plantation was set up.*
1843 *The U.S. recognized the Kingdom of Hawaii.*
1887 *King Kalakaua granted the United States rights to use Pearl Harbor as a naval base.*
1894 *The Republic of Hawaii was established after Queen Liliuokalani had been deposed in 1893.*
1898 *The United Nations annexed Hawaii.*
1900 *The United States created the Territory of Hawaii.*
1959 *Hawaii became the 50th state of the Union.*
1990 *A hurricane caused much damage, notably on Kauai.*

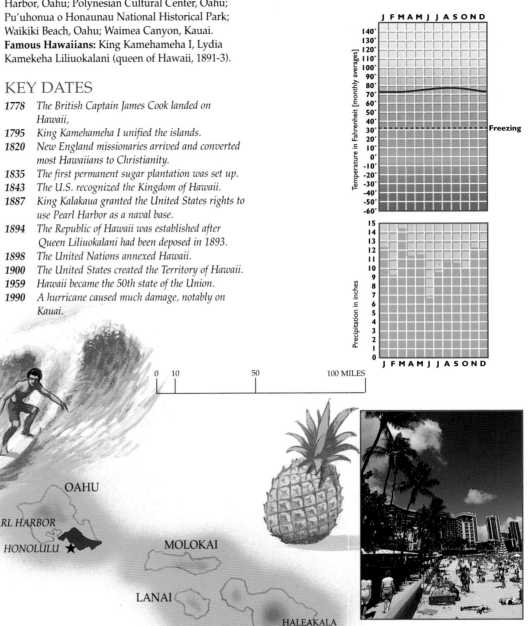

HAWAII
Station: HONOLULU

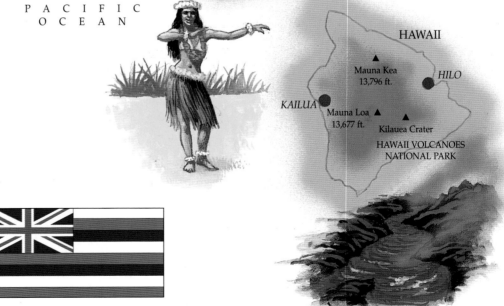

Waikiki beach, Oahu.

Idaho

Idaho, one of the Rocky Mountain States, is often called the Gem State. It ranks 13th in area but 41st in population.

Area: 83,564 sq. miles (216,430 sq.km.).
Population (1995): 1,163,261. *Urban:* 54%; *rural:* 46%.
Capital: Boise.
Largest cities (1990 census): Boise (125,551), Pocatello (46,117), Idaho Falls (43,673).
State motto: *Esto Perpetua* (Let it be perpetual)
State song: "Here We Have Idaho."
State symbols: *Flower:* syringa; *bird:* mountain bluebird; *tree:* western white pine.
Land features: Ranges of the Rocky Mountains make up most of central and northern Idaho, including the panhandle in the far north. The Rockies contain Borah Peak, the state's highest point at 12,662 ft. (3,859 m.). The Columbia plateau, which covers most of southern Idaho, is drained by the Snake River. West of Boise, this river turns north and forms part of the state's western border. Idaho's second largest river, the Salmon, flows into the Snake River in the northwest. The southeast contains part of the Basin and Range region, with mountains, plateaus and deep valleys. Forests cover about two-fifths of the land.
Climate: Much of Idaho has cold winters and warm, dry summers, though the mountains are much cooler. Much of the precipitation falls as snow.
Economy: Idaho is rich in natural resources, including forests, fertile soil, minerals, and its large water supplies, which are used to produce electricity and to irrigate the land. Manufactures include processed foods, wood products, and machinery, including computers and farm equipment. Farmland covers about a fourth of the land. Potatoes, hay, and wheat are leading crops. Beef cattle are raised on ranches, while dairy farms are located in the south. Gold, phosphate rock (used to make fertilizer), and silver are all mined. Service industries account for two-thirds of the state's gross product.
Major attractions: Part of Yellowstone National Park straddles the border with Wyoming in the east. Idaho also contains the Craters of the Moon National Monument, west of Idaho Falls; the Nez Percé National Historical Park near Lewiston; and the Sawtooth National Recreation Area in south-central Idaho. Other natural attractions include Crystal Ice Cave, near Pocatello; Hell's Canyon, the deepest gorge in North America, on the Snake River; Shoshone Falls, near Twin Falls; and Sun Valley, a resort nearly 100 miles (160 km.) east of Boise.
Famous Idahoans: Gutzon Borglum, Ezra Pound. Sacagawea (or Sacajawea).

KEY DATES

1805 The explorers Meriwether Lewis and William Clark were the first Europeans to explore the area.
1809 The first fur-trading post in Idaho was opened.
1834 Fort Boise and Fort Hall were established.
1863 Idaho Territory was established.
1877 Led by Chief Joseph, the Nez Percé, who were resisting attempts to make them move from Oregon to Idaho, were defeated by U.S. troops in a battle in north-central Idaho.
1890 Idaho became the 43rd state of the Union.
1959 Brownlee Dam, the first major hydroelectric dam on the Snake River, was completed.

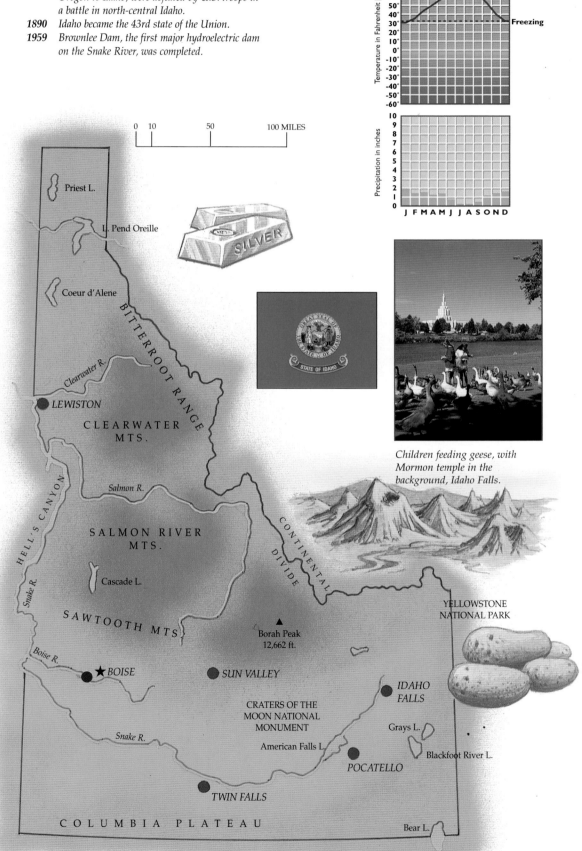

Children feeding geese, with Mormon temple in the background, Idaho Falls.

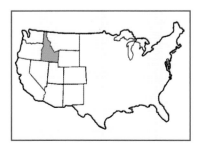

Montana

Montana, one of the Rocky Mountain States, was nicknamed the Treasure State after its reserves of gold and silver. It ranks 4th in area, but only 44th in population.

Area: 147,046 sq. miles (380,847 sq. km.).
Population (1995): 870,281. *Urban:* 53%; *rural:* 47%.
Capital: Helena.
Largest cities (1990 census): Billings (81,125), Great Falls (55,125), Missoula (42,918), Butte (33,326), Helena (24,609).
State motto: *Oro y Plata* (Gold and silver).
State song: "Montana."
State symbols: *Flower:* bitterroot; *bird:* western meadowlark; *tree:* Ponderosa pine.
Land features: Eastern Montana is part of the gently rolling Great Plains, though some mountain areas rise above the generally flat land. The Rocky Mountains make up western Montana and include the state's highest point, Granite Peak, which reaches 12,799 ft. (3,901 m.) near the southern border with Wyoming. The major rivers include the Missouri and its tributary, the Yellowstone River. Forests cover about a quarter of the area.
Climate: The Great Plains have cold winters and warm summers, but temperatures are lower in the high Rocky Mountains. However, the eastern slopes of the Rockies sometimes have mild winters because of a wind called the chinook. This wind flows down the mountainsides, getting warmer as it descends and can raise the temperature by 1°F for every 180 ft. (1°C for every 99 m.) in the space of minutes. The chinook melts the snow, allowing farmers to graze their herds. However, where it does not occur, winters are harsh. The rainfall is moderate on the Great Plains, but it is much higher in many mountain areas.
Economy: Natural resources include plenty of farmland, forests and minerals, notably coal, oil and several metal ores. Farmland covers about two-thirds of Montana. Beef cattle, dairy cattle, and sheep are all important, while wheat, barley, and hay are major crops. Wood products are the leading manufactures, followed by processed foods. However, service industries account for about four-fifths of the state's gross product.
Major attractions: Big Hole National Battlefield, in southwestern Montana; Glacier National Park in the northwest; Little Bighorn Battlefield National Monument, east of Billings; Medicine Rocks, in the badlands of southeastern Montana; Virginia City, near Dillon; Yellowstone National Park has three entrances in Montana, though most of the park is in Wyoming.
Famous Montanans: Gary Cooper, Jeanette Rankin.

**MONTANA
Station: HELENA**

KEY DATES

1740s	*French trappers may have reached the area.*
1803	*Eastern Montana became part of the United States because of the Louisiana Purchase.*
1805	*The explorers William Clark and Meriwether Lewis crossed the area on their way to the Pacific coast.*
1864	*The Montana Territory was created.*
1876	*U.S. troops were defeated at the Battle of the Little Bighorn.*
1877	*The Nez Percé Indians surrendered to U.S. troops.*
1889	*Montana became the 41st state of the Union.*
1910	*Glacier National Park was established.*

Glacier National Park.

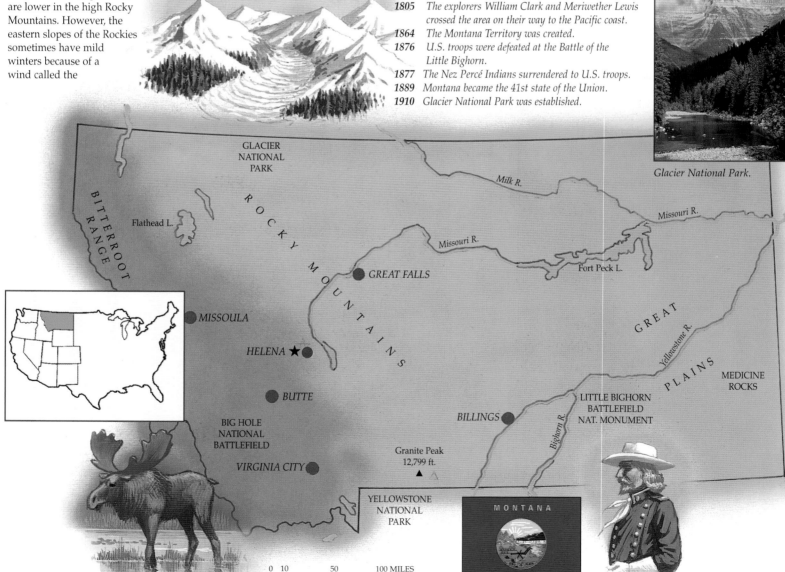

Nevada

Nevada, one of the Rocky Mountain States, was nicknamed the Silver State for the silver that was once mined there. It is the 7th largest state, but ranks 38th in population.

Area: 110,561 sq. miles (286,352 sq. km.).
Population (1995): 1,530,108. *Urban: 85%; rural: 15%.*
Capital: Carson City.
Largest cities (1990 census): Las Vegas (258,204); Reno (133,850).
State motto: All for Our Country.
State song: "Home Means Nevada."
State symbols: *Flower*: sagebrush; *bird*: mountain bluebird; *tree*: bristlecone pine and single-leaf piñon.
Land features: Nevada is dominated by a series of mountains and basins that run generally from north to south. The highest point is Boundary Peak, which reaches 13,140 ft. (4,005 m.) south-east of Carson City, near the border with California. Most of the state's rivers dry up and do not reach the sea. For example, the Humboldt, Nevada's longest river, flows into a basin where the water is evaporated by the sun. Trees grow on mountainsides, but most of Nevada is desert.
Climate: The climate varies greatly from place to place. For example, while winters are cold in high mountain areas, southern Nevada has mild winters. Summers are hot in lowlying areas, but the mountains have cooler summers. The average rainfall in much of Nevada is less than 10 inches (254 mm.) per year, though some mountain areas have more than 20 inches (508 mm.).

Economy: Las Vegas, Reno, and Lake Tahoe are major areas of tourism and service industries (including many services for tourists), and account for four-fifths of the state's gross product. Because of the dry climate, farming is restricted to about one-eighth of the state. Much of this land is used for cattle and sheep ranching. Irrigation is important and hay, grown to feed cattle, is the leading crop. Mining is important and Nevada produces gold, silver, and oil. Manufactures include computers and parts for electronic equipment.
Major attractions: Great Basin National Park, in east-central Nevada; Hoover Dam; Lake Mead National Recreation Area; Lake Tahoe; Las Vegas and Reno gambling casinos; Virginia City, a ghost town.
Famous Nevadans: Wovokah, a Paiute and founder of the Ghost Dance religion.

KEY DATES

1776 *A Spanish missionary may have reached Nevada.*
1848 *The United States obtained the Nevada region at the end of the Mexican War.*
1859 *Silver was discovered at Virginia City and many prospectors entered the area.*
1861 *The Nevada Territory was created.*
1864 *Nevada became the 36th state of the Union.*
1931 *Gambling was legalized in Nevada.*
1936 *Hoover Dam (then called Boulder Dam) was completed.*
1951 *The Atomic Energy Commission began nuclear tests in Nevada.*

NEVADA
Station: LAS VEGAS

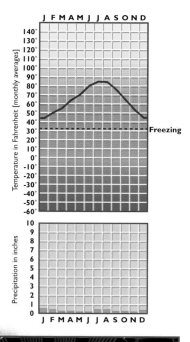

Las Vegas neon signs on The Strip.

BLACK ROCK DESERT

Humboldt R.

Pyramid L.

RENO

VIRGINIA CITY

L. Tahoe ★ CARSON CITY

Walker L.

SHOSHONE MTS.

GREAT BASIN

GREAT BASIN NATIONAL PARK

Boundary Peak 13,140 ft.

DEATH VALLEY NATIONAL PARK

Meadow Valley Wash

LAS VEGAS

HOOVER DAM LAKE MEAD NATIONAL RECREATION AREA

Colorado R.

L. Mohave

0 10   50   100 MILES

Red Rock Canyon, Nevada.

New Mexico

New Mexico, in the southwest, is nicknamed the Land of Enchantment because of its natural beauty and historic associations. It is the 5th largest state, but ranks 36th in population.

Area: 121,593 sq. miles (314,924 sq. km.).
Population (1995): 1,685,401. *Urban:* 72%; *rural:* 28%.
Capital: Santa Fe.
Largest cities (1990 census): Albuquerque (384,619), Las Cruces (62,360), Santa Fe (56,537).
State motto: *Crescit Eundo* (It grows as it goes).
State song: "O, Fair New Mexico."
State symbols: *Flower:* yucca flower; *bird:* roadrunner; *tree:* piñon, or nut pine.
Land features: The southern ranges of the Rocky Mountains extend into north-central New Mexico. These ranges include the state's highest point, Wheeler Peak, which reaches 13,161 ft. (4,011 m.). The northeast contains part of the Colorado Plateau, while the Great Plains occupy eastern New Mexico. The southwest is a region of mountain ranges that overlook deep basins. The state's chief rivers are the Rio Grande and the Pecos. Forests cover about a quarter of the land.
Climate: Winters in New Mexico are mild and summers are hot, especially in the south, which attracts retired people from other parts of the United States. The precipitation, including rain and melted snow, is generally low. The south and center contain deserts, with an average precipitation of less than 10 inches (254 mm.) per year.
Economy: New Mexico's chief resources include oil and natural gas, coal, copper, molybdenum, and potash. Much of the state has poor soils and cattle ranching is the main type of farming. Crops, grown mainly on irrigated land, include cotton, hay, grain sorghum, pecans, and wheat. Manufactures include electrical and electronic equipment and processed food products. However, service industries account for about seven-tenths of the state's gross product.
Major attractions: Carlsbad Caverns National Park, in the southeast; Chaco Culture National Historical Park, near Farmington; Los Alamos Bradbury Science Hall and Museum. The state also has several National Monuments, including Aztec Ruins in the northwest; Bandelier in north-central New Mexico; Capulin Volcano in the northeast; Gila Cliff Dwellings in the southwest; and White Sands in south-central New Mexico.
Famous New Mexicans: Geronimo, Conrad N. Hilton, Bill Mauldin.

KEY DATES

1540-2 *The Spaniard Vásquez de Coronado explored the area that is now New Mexico.*
1598 *The first permanent Spanish settlement was founded northwest of the present site of Santa Fe.*
1821 *Mexico became independent from Spain and New Mexico became a Mexican province.*
1848 *New Mexico became part of the United States following the Mexican War (1846-48).*
1850 *The Territory of New Mexico was created.*
1886 *Geronimo surrendered, ending the Apache Wars.*
1912 *New Mexico became the 47th state.*
1945 *The first atomic bomb was exploded at Trinity Site, near Alamogordo.*

LEFT: Adobe houses, Acoma Pueblo.

NEW MEXICO
Station: SANTA FE

Freezing

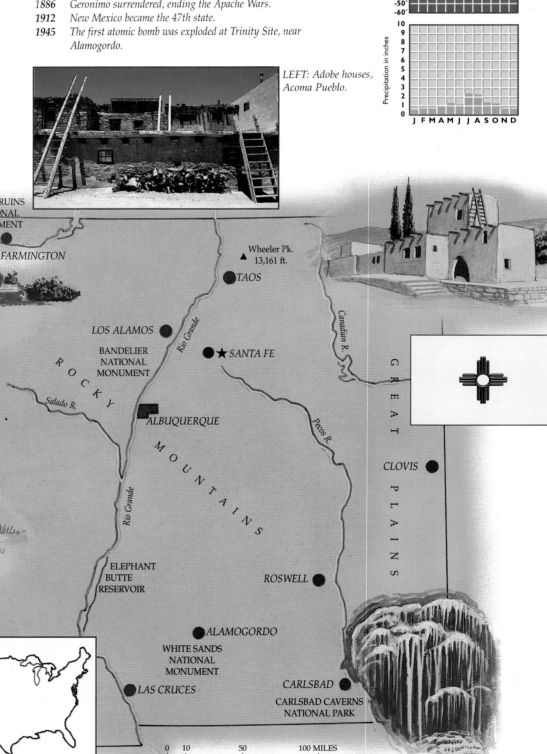

FOUR CORNERS
AZTEC RUINS NATIONAL MONUMENT
San Juan R.
FARMINGTON
Wheeler Pk. 13,161 ft.
TAOS
Rio Grande
Canadian R.
LOS ALAMOS
BANDELIER NATIONAL MONUMENT
★ SANTA FE
R O C K Y
Salado R.
ALBUQUERQUE
Pecos R.
CLOVIS
Rio Grande
M O U N T A I N S
G R E A T   P L A I N S
GILA CLIFF DWELLINGS NATIONAL MONUMENT
ELEPHANT BUTTE RESERVOIR
ROSWELL
ALAMOGORDO
WHITE SANDS NATIONAL MONUMENT
LAS CRUCES
CARLSBAD
CARLSBAD CAVERNS NATIONAL PARK

0   10   50   100 MILES

Oregon

Oregon, one of the Pacific Coast States, was called the Beaver State for the beavers that were hunted for their furs in the state's early days. Oregon ranks 10th in area but only 29th in population.

Area: 97,073 sq. miles (251,418 sq. km.).
Population (1995): 3,140,585. *Urban:* 68%; *rural:* 32%.
Capital: Salem.
Largest cities (1990 census): Portland (438,802), Eugene (112,773), Salem (107,793), Gresham (68,249).
State motto: *Alis Volat Propriis* (She flies with her own wings).
State song: "Oregon, My Oregon."
State symbols: *Flower:* Oregon grape; *bird:* western meadowlark; *tree:* Douglas fir.
Land features: Oregon has much majestic scenery. The Cascade Mountains, which contain towering volcanic peaks, run north-south through western Oregon. They include the state's highest peak, Mount Hood, at 11,239 ft. (3,426 m.). West of the Cascade Mountains lie the Klamath Mountains in the southwest, the Coast Ranges bordering the Pacific Ocean, and the Willamette River valley, a small lowland area. East of the Cascade Mountains is the Columbia Plateau, although the southeast is a region of mountain ranges and basins. The chief river is the Columbia, which forms much of Oregon's boundary with Washington. Forests cover nearly half of the state.
Climate: Western Oregon has a mild climate, but the interior has cold winters and hot summers. The precipitation is greatest in the west and lowest in the east.
Economy: Oregon's natural resources include its forests and abundant water supplies. The most important trees commercially are the Douglas fir and the Ponderosa pine. The processing of lumber is the chief manufacturing industry, followed by food processing. Beef and dairy cattle are raised and milk is a leading farm product. The chief crop is wheat, but barley, hay, and oats are also important. Greenhouse and nursery products,

including bulbs, together with fruit and vegetables, are also produced. However, service industries account for about three-quarters of the state's gross product.
Major attractions: Columbia River Gorge, in the Cascade Mountains; Crater Lake National Park; Fort Clatsop National Memorial, near Astoria in the northwest; John Day Fossil Beds National Monument, in north-central Oregon; McLoughlin House National Historic Site, near Portland; Oregon Caves National Monument southwest of Medford.
Famous Oregonians: Edwin Markham, Linus Pauling, John Reed.

KEY DATES

1579 The Englishman Sir Francis Drake may have reached the coast of what is now Oregon.
1805 The explorers Meriwether Lewis and William Clark reach the mouth of the Columbia River.
1846 A treaty fixed the 49th parallel as the main boundary between U.S. and British territory.
1840s Settlers moved west to the Willamette valley along the Oregon Trail.
1848 Oregon became a Territory.
1859 Oregon became the 33rd state of the Union.
1937 Bonneville Dam was completed, supplying electricity for industry.

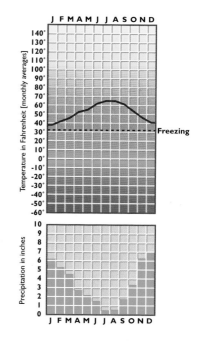

OREGON
Station: PORTLAND

Crater Lake, Oregon.

ASTORIA

Columbia R.

PORTLAND

GRESHAM

BLUE MOUNTAINS

JOHN DAY FOSSIL BEDS NATIONAL MONUMENT

John Day R.

Mt. Hood 11,239 ft.

Deschutes R.

SALEM

COLUMBIA PLATEAU

Snake R.

PACIFIC OCEAN

COAST RANGES

Willamette R.

EUGENE

CASCADE MTS.

CRATER LAKE NATIONAL PARK

Owyhee R.

Rogue R.

MEDFORD

KLAMATH MTS.

GREAT BASIN

STATE OF OREGON

1859

0 10   50   100 MILES

Utah

Utah is nicknamed the Beehive State, after the Mormon name for the area, Deseret, meaning "honey bee." One of the Rocky Mountain States, Utah is the 11th largest state, but ranks 34th in population.

Area: 84,899 sq. miles (219,887 sq. km.).
Population (1995): 1,951,408. *Urban:* 84%; *rural:* 16%.
Capital: Salt Lake City.
Largest cities: Salt Lake City (159,928), West Valley City (close to Salt Lake and not shown on the map, 86,969), Provo (86,835).
State motto: Industry.
State song: "Utah, We Love Thee."
State symbols: *Flower:* sego lily; *bird:* sea gull; *tree:* blue spruce.
Land features: Utah has much spectacular scenery. Part of the Rocky Mountains extends into northeastern Utah and this region contains the state's highest point, Kings Peak, which reaches 13,528 ft. (4,123 m.). The state's largest region is the Colorado Plateau, which covers most of the south and the east. The west is a region of mountain ranges separating deep basins. Great Salt Lake occupies one of the basins. Deserts cover about a third of the land and forests another 30%.
Climate: Most of Utah has hot summers and mild winters, with a low average yearly precipitation. However, the northeastern mountains have warm summers and cold winters, with plenty of rain and snow.
Economy: Utah's natural resources include oil, coal, natural gas, uranium, and copper. Most soils are poor, but farmers raise beef and dairy cattle. Most cropland is irrigated. The leading crop is hay, while barley, corn, and wheat are also important. Fruit, vegetables, and greenhouse and nursery products are also grown. Manufactures include transportation equipment, processed food products, scientific instruments, and printed materials. However, service industries account for about three-quarters of the state's gross product.
Major attractions: Southern Utah contains five national parks – Arches, Bryce Canyon, Canyonlands, Capitol Reef, and Zion – while the state's national monuments include Cedar Breaks, Dinosaur, Natural Bridges, and Timpanogos Cave. Other attractions include Beehive House and the Mormon Temple, Salt Lake City; Bonneville Salt Flats in the northwest; the Glen Canyon National Recreation Area, including Lake Powell, in the south; Golden Spike National Historic Site in the northwest; Great Salt Lake; Monument Valley in the southeast.
Famous Utahans: Maude Adams, John Moses Browning, Philo Farnsworth, J. Willard Marriot, Brigham Young.

KEY DATES

1540 *Spanish explorers reached the area that is now Utah.*
1847 *Brigham Young, leading the first Mormon pioneers, reached the Great Salt Lake area.*
1849 *The Mormons created the state of Deseret.*
1850 *The Territory of Utah was created.*
1869 *The first transcontinental railroad was completed when lines from the east and west met in Utah.*
1896 *Utah became the 45th state of the Union.*
1952 *Uranium was discovered at Moab.*
1956 *Water supplies were increased with the completion of dams in the northeast and south.*

Capitol, Salt Lake City.

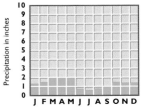

UTAH
Station: SALT LAKE CITY

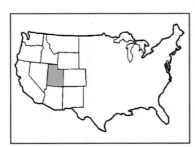

BONNEVILLE SALT FLATS

DESERT

Bear L.

Bear R.

Great Salt Lake

● OGDEN

★ SALT LAKE CITY

Kings Pk. ▲ 13,528 ft.

DINOSAUR NATIONAL MONUMENT

TOOELE ● TIMPANOGOS CAVE NAT. MONUMENT

Uinta R.

Utah L. ● PROVO

Duchesne R.

GREAT SALT LAKE

WASATCH RANGE

TAVAPUTS PLATEAU

Green R.

Price R.

San Rafael R.

Sevier L.

COLORADO PLATEAU

Dirty Devil R.

ARCHES NATIONAL PARK

Colorado R.

Sevier R.

CAPITOL REEF NATIONAL PARK

CANYONLANDS NATIONAL PARK

GLEN CANYON NATIONAL RECREATION AREA

NATURAL BRIDGES NATIONAL MONUMENT

BRYCE CANYON NATIONAL PARK

CEDAR BREAKS NATIONAL MONUMENT

San Juan R.

ZION NATIONAL PARK

L. Powell

MONUMENT VALLEY

FOUR CORNERS

0 10   50   100 MILES

Washington

Washington is one of the Pacific Coast States. Nicknamed the Evergreen State for its huge evergreen forests, it is the 20th largest state and ranks 15th in population.

Area: 68,139 sq. miles (176,479 sq. km.).
Population (1995): 5,430,940. *Urban:* 74%; *rural:* 26%.
Capital: Olympia.
Largest cities: Seattle (516,259), Spokane (177,165), Tacoma (176,664), Bellevue (close to Seattle and not shown on the map, 86,872), Everett (69,974).
State motto: *Alki* (Bye and bye).
State song: "Washington, My Home."
State symbols: *Flower:* coast rhododendron; *bird:* willow goldfinch; *tree:* western hemlock.
Land features: Much of Washington is mountainous. Part of the Rocky Mountains is in the northeast, while the Columbia Plateau lies in the southeast. The Cascade Range runs north-south through west-central Washington. This range includes the state's highest peak, a volcano called Mount Rainier, which reaches 14,410 ft. (4,392 m.). Another volcano in the range is Mount St. Helens at 8,364 ft. (2,549 m.). West of this volcanic range is the Puget Sound lowland, with the Olympic Mountains in the northwest, and the Coast Ranges in the southwest. The chief river is the Columbia which forms much of the state's southern border. Forests cover about half of the state.
Climate: Western Washington has a mild climate, with warm summers and mild winters, but the climate is more extreme to the east. The precipitation, including rain and melted snow, is heavy in the west, but it decreases to the east. Part of the Columbia plateau is desert.

Economy: Abundant water supplies and forests are the chief natural resources. Many dams, such as the huge Grand Coulee, and hydroelectric plants have been built on the rivers and they produce most of the state's electric supply. Douglas fir and western hemlock are the most valuable trees, and paper and wood products are the third most important manufactures, after transportation equipment and processed food products. Major crops include hops, potatoes and wheat, while apples, beef cattle and milk are other valuable products. However, service industries account for more than seven-tenths of the state's gross product.
Major attractions: Fort Vancouver National Historic Site, in the southwest; Grand Coulee Dam; Mount Rainier National Park; Mount St. Helens National Volcanic Monument; North Cascades National Park; Olympic National Park; Space Needle, Seattle; Whitman Mission National Historic Site, in the southeast.
Famous Washingtonians: Bing Crosby, Mary McCarthy, Edward R. Murrow.

KEY DATES

1775   *Spanish explorers reached the coast.*
1805   *William Clark and Meriwether Lewis reached Washington after crossing the Rocky Mountains.*
1853   *Washington Territory was created.*
1883   *Washington was linked to the eastern United States by the Northern Pacific Railroad.*
1889   *Washington became the 42nd state of the Union.*
1942   *The Grand Coulee Dam was completed.*
1980   *Mount St. Helens in the Cascade Mountains erupted with great force, killing 57 people.*

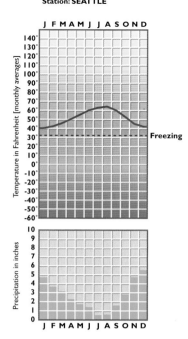

WASHINGTON
Station: SEATTLE

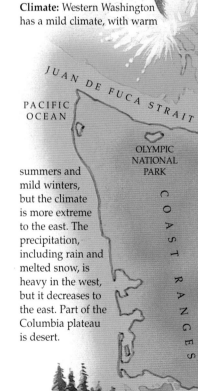

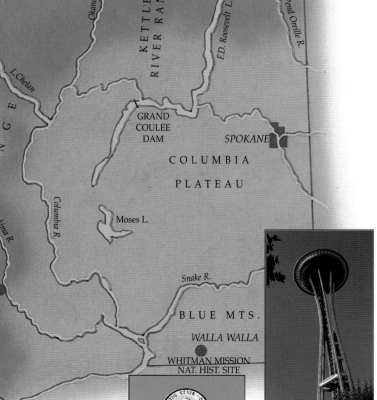

Space Needle, Seattle.

Wyoming

Wyoming, one of the Rocky Mountain States, is nicknamed the Equality State, because women were given the vote in 1869, earlier than in any other state. Wyoming is the 9th largest, but has the smallest population of any of the 50 states.

Area: 97,809 sq. miles (253,325 sq. km.).
Population (1995): 480,184. *Urban:* 63%; *rural:* 37%.
Capital: Cheyenne.
Largest cities: Cheyenne (50,008); Casper (46,765), Laramie (26,687).
State motto: Equal Rights.
State song: "Wyoming."
State symbols: *Flower:* Indian paintbrush; *bird:* meadowlark; *tree:* cottonwood.
Land features: Ranges of the Rocky Mountains cover much of the state. One of them, the Wind River Range, contains the state's highest point, Gannett Peak, which reaches 13,804 ft. (4,207 m.). Between several of the ranges lie fairly flat basins. In the east lie the Great Plains, although part of the Black Hills of South Dakota extend into northeastern Wyoming. The state contains parts of three river systems: tributaries of the Missouri River flow north and east, the Green River in the southwest flows into Utah, and the Snake River in the northwest flows west to join the Columbia River. Forests cover about a sixth of the state.

Climate: Wyoming has cold winters and warm summers. Part of the state, especially in the basins between the mountains, are dry and the land is desert. But the average yearly precipitation, including rain and melted snow, is around 50 inches (1270 mm.) in the northwest.
Economy: Wyoming's natural resources, which include oil, natural gas (as well as coal and mining), are the state's most valuable industries. Wyoming has large areas of grazing land and farmers raise beef cattle and sheep on huge ranches. Milk and wool are important products. Much of the cropland is irrigated and major crops include barley, corn, hay, sugar beets, and wheat. Manufacturing plays a fairly small part in the state's economy. The chief industries are the manufacture of chemical products and oil refining. Service industries account for about two-thirds of the state's gross product.
Major attractions: Devils Tower National Monument, in the northeast; Flaming Gorge National Recreation Site; Fort Laramie National Historic Site, in the northwest; Fossil Butte National Monument in the southwest; Frontier Days Celebration in Cheyenne every June; Grand Teton National Park, south of Yellowstone; Yellowstone National Park.
Famous Wyomingites: Jackson Pollock, Spotted Tail (leader of the Brulé Sioux).

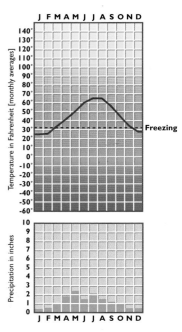

WYOMING
Station: CHEYENNE

KEY DATES

1807 A trapper, John Colter, became the first white man to reach the Yellowstone area.
1868 Wyoming Territory was created.
1869 The Union Pacific Railroad reached Wyoming.
1872 Yellowstone was made a national park, the first in the United States.

1883 The first oil well was drilled in Wyoming.
1890 Wyoming became the 44th state of the Union.
1906 Devils Tower became the first national monument.
1960 Wyoming became the headquarters of the country's first long-range missile squadron.

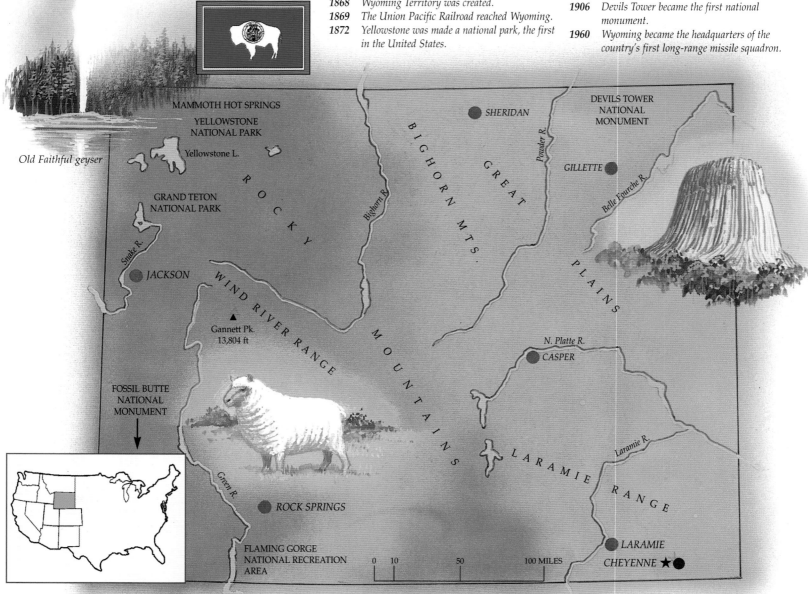

Old Faithful geyser

MAMMOTH HOT SPRINGS
YELLOWSTONE NATIONAL PARK
Yellowstone L.
GRAND TETON NATIONAL PARK
Snake R.
JACKSON
Gannett Pk. 13,804 ft
WIND RIVER RANGE
FOSSIL BUTTE NATIONAL MONUMENT
Green R.
ROCK SPRINGS
FLAMING GORGE NATIONAL RECREATION AREA

SHERIDAN
BIGHORN MTS.
Bighorn R.
Powder R.
GREAT
PLAINS
ROCKY MOUNTAINS
N. Platte R.
CASPER
LARAMIE RANGE
Laramie R.
LARAMIE
CHEYENNE ★ ●

DEVILS TOWER NATIONAL MONUMENT
GILLETTE
Belle Fourche R.

0 10   50   100 MILES

Old Faithful geyser, Yellowstone National Park, Wyoming.